THE SOLDIER THROUGH THE AGES

THE GREEK HOPLITE

Martin Windrow

Illustrated by
Tony Smith

Franklin Watts
London   New York   Toronto   Sydney

First printed in Great Britain in 1985 by
Franklin Watts Ltd
12a Golden Square
London W1

First published in the USA by
Franklin Watts Inc.
387 Park Avenue South
New York
N.Y. 10016

First published in Australia by
Franklin Watts Australia
1 Campbell Street
Artarmon
NSW 2064

UK ISBN: 0 86313 154 9
US ISBN: 0-531-03780-0
Library of Congress Catalog Card Number: 84-50020

Designed by James Marks
Cover illustration by Gerry Embleton

Printed in Belgium

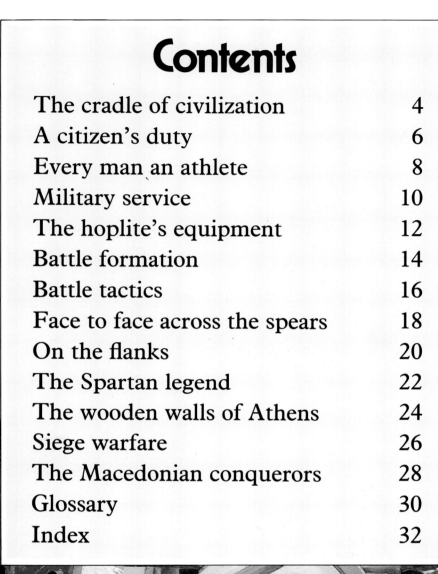

Contents

The cradle of civilization	4
A citizen's duty	6
Every man an athlete	8
Military service	10
The hoplite's equipment	12
Battle formation	14
Battle tactics	16
Face to face across the spears	18
On the flanks	20
The Spartan legend	22
The wooden walls of Athens	24
Siege warfare	26
The Macedonian conquerors	28
Glossary	30
Index	32

The cradle of civilization

The civilization which is called Classical Greece occupied the lands around the Aegean Sea in the 6th and 5th centuries BC. It was the earliest European civilization which left full written records for historians, and its art, politics, culture and its armies were far more advanced than those found anywhere else in the West.

Ancient Greece was never a single unified country. Because the countryside was mostly mountainous and wooded, there were few places where people could settle to farm good land. As a result, the towns that were built were far apart, and grew up into separate city-states, covering fairly small areas. The city-states were constantly quarreling and forming alliances in rivalry with one another. This rivalry often led to open warfare, particularly between the armies of the city-states of Athens and Sparta.

In the Classical period the infantryman was the backbone of all the armies of the different Greek states. He was called a hoplite, which means an armored man. The hoplite fought in an organized regiment of men, each of whom used the same weapons in the same way. He was given military training according to rules laid down by his government.

▷ A typical Greek heavy infantryman of the two centuries between 600 and 400 BC. The Greek hoplite wore a crested bronze helmet. His chest and back were protected by armor of metal or heavy fabric, and on his legs he wore metal greaves. He was armed with a long spear which he used for stabbing, not throwing.

The Greek hoplite was a disciplined fighter, obeying the orders of his officers, at a time when other warriors in Europe fought as loose mobs of undisciplined individuals. As far as we know, the Greek hoplite was the first European who was not just a warrior but a soldier. He and his fellow fighters were the true ancestors of today's armies.

◁ The most important Greek city-states of the 6th and 5th centuries are shown on this map. The rivalry between Athens and Sparta led to a long series of ruinous wars. In the end this so weakened them that they were ripe for invasion from the strong new kingdom of Macedonia in the north.

A citizen's duty

The Greek hoplite was not a full-time, paid soldier. Usually he earned his living as a farmer: rich men lived in the city and had stewards to run their estates, while poorer men worked their land themselves. All citizens, rich or poor, also played a part in running their city by voting in the city assembly. And, in times of war, rich and poor alike were expected to report for army service.

Citizens had the time for these duties because almost everyone owned slaves. These might be foreign prisoners or poor people who had been sold into slavery when they could not pay their debts. There were many more slaves than citizens, and they did all heavy work. A rich man might own as many as 1,000 slaves, and even a poor peasant farmer had two or three.

In Athens there was a third class of people, called metics. These were foreigners living in the city. They were mostly businessmen and traders. They had few political rights, but they did serve in the army. In all, Athens is believed to have had about 40,000 citizens, plus their families; 20,000 metics, and their families; and about 180,000 slaves.

▷ The three "faces" of an Athenian citizen: soldier, voter and farmer. Every healthy male citizen was expected to serve in the army whenever he was needed. The Greeks believed that if a man enjoyed the advantages of living in a city, then he should be prepared to fight to defend it.

The citizen was also expected to attend the city assembly regularly – perhaps three times a month – and to help run the city by electing officials and passing laws.

Most farmers did not have enough flat land to grow much grain. Instead they grew grapes for wine, and olives, the two crops that made Athens rich. They also grew many different kinds of vegetables.

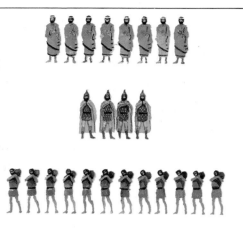

△ For every eight citizens of Athens (top), there were about four metics, (middle), and twelve slaves (bottom). The Athenian army in about 430 BC was made up of about 13,000 citizen hoplites; 9,500 metics; 1,400 young cadets; 2,500 veterans in their 50s, and 1,000 wealthy men on horseback – a total of 27,400 men.

Every man an athlete

A Greek boy's education was decided by his father. Usually he was sent to take lessons at the house of a paid teacher, often accompanied by one of his father's slaves, who made sure he did not play truant! In a small class of other boys, he was taught reading, writing, poetry, arithmetic and music.

In a country where every man was a part-time soldier, and at a time when soldiers fought with heavy iron-bladed weapons, it was important for each boy to grow up strong and agile. From about the age of twelve Greek boys were sent for regular training at an athletics school.

The school had an open-air training ground surrounded by changing-rooms, baths and offices. The earth of the training ground was regularly dug, raked and watered to keep it soft. Here, under the eye of the instructor, boys practiced fitness exercises, jumping, wrestling, throwing the discus and javelin, and boxing. (Boxing in ancient Greece was a tough sport, since the boxers used heavy straps wrapped round their fists instead of today's padded gloves.)

After his education was completed, the young Greek man still took part in sports to keep himself in shape. In wartime his life would depend on his strength, endurance and quick reflexes.

▷ Greek boys practicing at an athletics school. The instructors wore purple robes and carried forked sticks. Flute-players helped the boys keep in time. For some exercises the boys carried weights to improve their strength and balance. When they wrestled, they covered themselves with oil and sand for grip. Each boy took his oil pot to school with him – and sponges and metal scrapers so that he could clean off this mess in the baths afterwards!

8

Military service

When he was eighteen, every Athenian boy reported for two years' full-time military training as a cadet. The cadets were formed into units according to their home district. Whenever he was called up for army service in later life, the soldier served in this same unit, made up of neighbors and friends of his own age. Officers were elected by the district's voters from among trusted veterans.

For the first year the cadets, dressed in special black cloth tunics, lived in barracks just outside Athens. First they were taught how to handle their weapons, wear their armor, and drill together. Since their families had to buy their armor, there was a good deal of difference from man to man.

During that first year the cadets were taken to all the important fortresses in the country so that they would know their way around if they ever had to defend them in wartime. At the end of the year the cadets put on a grand parade and drill display, and each one was presented by the city authorities with a shield and spear to mark his graduation.

For the second year the cadets garrisoned forts around the frontiers. Life was probably pleasant enough: they were used to exercise, an open-air life and a simple diet. (Most Greeks ate barley bread, with cheese, fish, olives, onions and other vegetables, and pork or goat for special occasions.)

The cadet returned to private life when he was twenty; but he could be recalled to the army in wartime at any time up to his sixtieth birthday. Men in their fifties were called up to garrison the forts alongside the cadets. Although the part-time citizen-soldier was given no pay for his service, he received free medical attention if he was wounded, and a public pension.

▷ A young Athenian hoplite is helped into his armor by his father and brothers. His age-group has been called up for service with his district regiment. He will serve with the main army. His father and his younger brother – who wears the black tunic of a cadet – will serve as fort guards.

◁ The beautiful shield markings probably identified units, as well as being decorative. There were many types, including:

1 Gods or demons.
2 Real or imaginary animals.
3 Symbols or initial letters of city names.

The hoplite's equipment

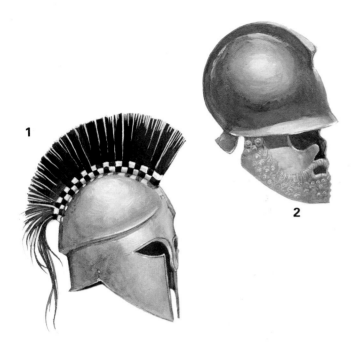

Helmets came in many styles, but most were bronze and covered the head except for narrow slots for the eyes, nose and mouth. As the metal was thin and springy, the helmet could be pushed up on top of the head when not in battle. Helmets were often embossed or painted for decoration, and were fitted with horsehair crests.

The hoplite wore a cuirass to protect his chest and back. In the 6th century BC this

◁ **1, 2** Two common helmet types, the Corinthian and Thracian. The latter has a beard embossed on the face-piece for decoration.

▽ **3** "Muscled" cuirass. **4** Linen cuirass; metal plates were sometimes added for extra protection. The cloth was about $\frac{1}{4}$ in (0.5 cm) thick.

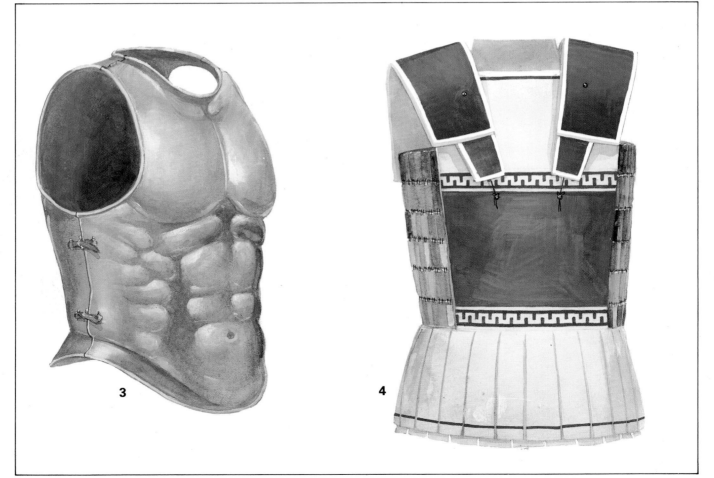

was bronze and "muscled" like a human torso. This elegant but expensive armor was later replaced by a simpler version made of layers of stiff cloth glued together. The legs were protected by greaves, flexible metal shin guards.

The hoplite carried a round shield made of wood covered with bronze which measured about 2 ft 7 in (80 cm) across. Its in-turned rim rested on his shoulder, taking some of the weight off his arm.

His main weapon was a long ash-wood spear with an iron blade. Often it had a spike at the butt end, to be used if the spear was broken in battle. Various types of short swords were also carried for close fighting.

▽ **5** Greaves, split up the back to fit around the legs.
6, 7 Inside and outside of the shield. A leather curtain was sometimes attached to stop arrows aimed at the legs.
8 Spear, between 5 and 8 ft (1.5 m–2.5 m) long.
9 The usual type of double-edged sword, about 2 ft (60 cm) long.
10 Another type of sword, the single-edged kopis, used like a cleaver.

Battle formation

The Greeks fought in tight-packed formations, so it was important for the hoplite to learn how to handle his awkward spear and shield without getting in his comrades' way. The diagram on the right shows the basic formation: a company of 100 men, drawn up 8 deep by 12 wide.

The smallest unit was the single file of 8 men, one behind the other. The senior man in each file stood at the front. Three files made up a platoon of 25 men (red, yellow, blue, brown). The extra, 25th, man was an experienced veteran, who stood behind the platoon to keep an eye on the men. The platoon commanders (the large colored figures) stood at the front of their right-hand file. The four platoons made up the company.

In battle the army used a very simple formation called the phalanx. All the 100-man companies simply stood side by side, in a long line 8 ranks deep. In a big battle the phalanx might be $1\frac{1}{4}$ miles (2 km) long from end to end.

▷ Hoplites in typical fighting positions:
1 Crouched behind the shield, sheltering against arrows.
2 Standing in the battle-line, thrusting underarm with the spear.
3 Thrusting overarm, perhaps over the shoulder of the man in front. The phalanx was too tightly packed for any more complicated movements.

1

2

3

15

Battle tactics

The important thing about the Greek hoplite was that he fought not just for himself, but as one of a team. The tactics of the phalanx worked because each soldier kept in his allotted place, acting together with his comrades, according to orders. This discipline held the phalanx together, so that each soldier could take advantage of opportunities to help the men on each side of him.

When two Greek armies met in battle, the lines were drawn up some distance apart. After the commanders had whipped up their men's courage with inspiring speeches, trumpets sounded the advance. To the sound of flutes and war songs, each mass of spearmen marched toward the other. At the last moment they broke into a run, and two opposing front ranks crashed together, shield to shield.

Each man stabbed with his spear, trying to reach past the shields of the men facing him. The men behind stabbed over the shoulders of the front rank. Those too far back to reach pushed on the backs of the men in front, or passed extra spears forward to them.

▷ The spearman's helmet covered most of his face. His shield covered his body from chin to thigh, and greaves protected his legs. But his right side was partly exposed to a spear thrust when he raised his right arm to stab downward with his own spear. For this reason, he tended to tuck himself well in behind the edge of the shield of the man on his right.

16

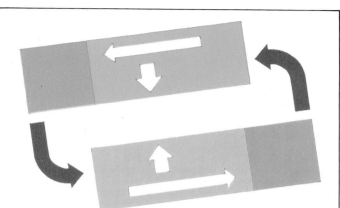

△ This is what often happened in a Greek battle. Each army usually put its best men at the right-hand end of its battle-line, so they often pushed back the weaker troops facing them. As both wings pushed forward, the whole battle started to turn counterclockwise.

Soldiers in both armies gradually shuffled to their right, trying to keep behind the shields of the men on their right. So the right-hand end of each battle-line soon overlapped the weaker left-hand end of the enemy line, and attacked it from the flank.

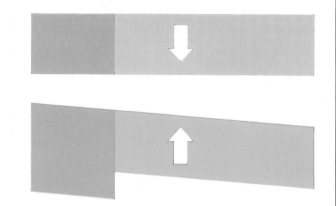

△ This is how a Theban general beat the Spartans at the Battle of Leuctra in 371 BC. The Thebans (green) advanced in a slanted line. Their best men were placed on the left, not on the right as usual; and they were drawn up in many more ranks than the rest of the army. So the strongest part of the Theban army hit the Spartans first; and, having so many ranks, they were able to beat the best of the Spartans. By the time the rest of the Theban line closed in on them, the Spartans were already crumbling.

Face to face across the spears

Two Greek armies crash together in the first moment of battle. Once the rigid lines of spearmen were locked in combat, there was little room for maneuver or cunning. The battle was decided by a vicious, face-to-face killing-match. This did not usually last long. Many of the officers, fighting in the front rank, fell early in the battle. Their men would be shaken; and once it was clear which side was winning, the losers often gave up and ran for their lives. They were usually allowed to get away. Once the victory had been won on the battlefield, it was thought dishonorable to hunt down beaten men and butcher them.

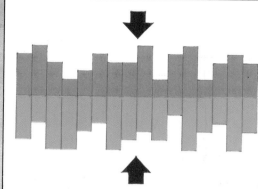

◁ Two armies locked in battle. As each man fell, the man behind stepped forward into his place. Eventually, one army would wear right through; as soon as the phalanx was broken, it was lost. Battles were savage, although brief. An army of 4,000 men might be left with 1,000 dead.

On the flanks

The Greek hoplite, in his rigid phalanx, was very successful in war – so long as his enemy was another Greek spearman fighting in the same way. But armies often had to march through mountains or forests, where the spearmen could not easily form up in their tight ranks. So light supporting troops were often used as well, both to raid and ambush enemies, and to guard against such attacks.

Some of these light troops were recruited from poor citizens who could not afford hoplite armor and weapons. All they needed were javelins – throwing spears – and perhaps light shields of wicker and leather. Often Greek cities hired foreign mercenaries, soldiers who would fight for whoever paid them. Various neighboring peoples became famous for their skills with different weapons, and were hired for that reason.

Thracians made good peltasts – agile, light-armed javelin-men. Archers were recruited on the island of Crete; and the island of Rhodes was famous for its slingers. Their simple, cheap leather slings could hurl a stone or lead bullet up to 380 yd (350 m) with deadly effect.

The Greek cities had few cavalry, so for scouting round their armies they hired mercenary horsemen. The best horse-archers were the Scythians. These were wild, nomadic tribesmen from the great plains north of the Black Sea. The flat countryside of Thessaly and Boeotia was also good for horse-breeding, and provided the Greeks with another type of cavalry, who used javelins.

▷ Different types of light mercenary troops watch from a hilltop as their main army enters a mountain pass.
1 Thracian peltasts took their name from the pelta, a crescent-shaped wickerwork shield.
2 Scythian horse-archers wore loose, brightly patterned tunics and trousers. Bows and arrows were carried together in a case slung from the belt.
3 Red tunics were the mark of the Cretan archers.
4 Light horsemen from Thessaly could be recognized by their broad sunhats and gaudy, patterned cloaks.

The Spartan legend

The Greek city-state of Sparta was quite unlike all the others. The Spartans became legendary as the finest soldiers in the Greek world, and were feared and respected far and wide. We still use the word "Spartan" to describe tough people who bear hardship without complaint.

Spartan life was devoted to the military virtues of courage, strength and endurance. Sparta was a grim, uncomfortable place ruled by brutal laws, and Spartans scorned all the gentle and pleasant things of life. Even their food was a test of endurance – their most famous dish was a disgusting broth made from blood and vinegar!

The Spartan citizen had only one trade: war. He was given a state-owned farm to support himself, but he never actually worked on his land. All work except soldiering was done by the local peasants called helots, who lived in cruel slavery. This allowed Spartan citizens to concentrate on a full-time military life.

From the age of seven to the age of sixty, a Spartan belonged to the army. He was taken from his mother as a little boy, and put into cold, uncomfortable barracks with other boys of his age. He lived with these companions all his life. Together they moved up through the classes of a harsh training system. At twenty they were taken into the army proper, but they were not allowed to vote, or to marry, until they were thirty.

▷ A Spartan warrior encourages two boys to fight during a winter training run. The proud marks of the warrior were the red cloak, and long, carefully dressed hair. The Spartan boy was treated harshly. He was educated only enough to understand simple written orders and to sing marching songs. All the rest of his training was devoted to building up his strength, courage and cunning. He was given only a single tunic, winter and summer, and when he was older he often went naked. His hair was cropped, and he was seldom allowed to bathe. His rations were small and unappetizing. This was to encourage him to steal and to be cunning; but if he was caught he was whipped for carelessness. At 16 he faced harsh tests of endurance. He was turned out alone to live as best he could in the wild; and finally, he had to stalk and murder a slave.

Even married men were expected to spend most of their time in barracks, not with their families. It was believed that this made a man more willing to risk his life in battle. Even the women were trained to be hard and uncaring. The traditional farewell of a Spartan woman to her husband or son as he marched off to war was "Come back carrying your shield, or on it." Since the shield was the first thing a man discarded if he was running away from a defeat, and since the dead were carried home on their shields, this meant simply: "Come home victorious, or not at all." Love and kindness were considered to be weaknesses.

The Spartans fought in the same way as all other hoplites, without any special methods or tricks. But man for man they were stronger, braver and more aggressive than their fellow Greeks. The Spartan would die where he stood rather than retreat.

The wooden walls of Athens

An important part of Athens' wealth in peace, and her strength in war, came from her large fleet – the so-called wooden walls of Athens. Athens built up a trading empire scattered all over the islands and coasts of the eastern Mediterranean. The merchant ships which used the trade routes provided the city with thousands of skilled sailors and oarsmen to man warships in times of trouble. These seamen and oarsmen were free citizens of the poorer classes, not slaves.

Greek warships were called galleys. They were long and slim, and powered mainly by banks of oars along the sides. They had a single square sail on a mast, but this was lowered before battle. The Greeks used oars to carry out maneuvers, rather than relying on the changeable wind near the shore, where most battles were fought. The oarsmen, arranged on three levels, pulled the ship along at speeds of about $5\frac{1}{2}$ mph (9 km/h). Each ship carried 170 oarsmen, 15 crew to manage the sail, anchor and steering-oars and about 16 hoplites and archers.

In battle, the tactic was to ram an enemy ship with the long, strengthened "beak" fitted low on the bows. Sometimes this was enough to sink the enemy ship, for galleys were not very strongly built. If the enemy stayed afloat, the hoplites and archers leaped across to the enemy's deck to fight hand-to-hand. In emergencies the sailors and oarsmen probably helped out too, wielding daggers and clubs.

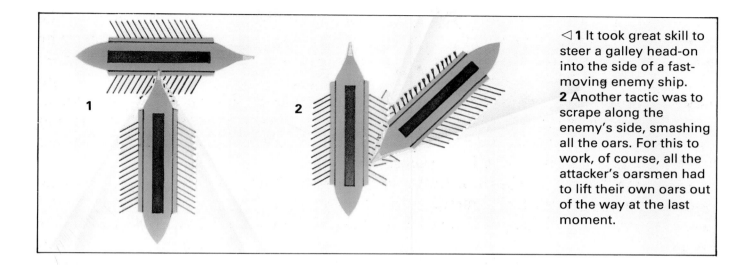

1 It took great skill to steer a galley head-on into the side of a fast-moving enemy ship.
2 Another tactic was to scrape along the enemy's side, smashing all the oars. For this to work, of course, all the attacker's oarsmen had to lift their own oars out of the way at the last moment.

▽ Greek and Persian galleys fighting each other in the Battle of Salamis, 480 BC. Athens put 200 ships into battle in this important victory – more than all other Greek navies added together.

Siege warfare

Greek armies of the 6th and 5th centuries BC used fairly simple methods to besiege an enemy city or fortress. First they built a circle of wooden fences and deep trenches all around it to cut off outside help and food supplies. Then the attackers settled down behind these ramparts and waited for the city to surrender. Often they simply bribed a traitor to open the gates.

If the Greeks decided to attack a fortified town, they raised great mounds of logs and earth against the outside of the walls. These provided ramps for storming parties to reach the top of the walls. Battering rams were sometimes used to break down the walls, and fire-arrows were aimed at wooden gates.

By the 4th century BC armies began to employ more powerful siege-machines. Great wooden catapults, powered by thick springs of twisted rope, were used to hurl stones at city walls. Battering rams were

▽ Greek fortress wall in about 400 BC. The two "skins" of stonework had rubble filling between them. Once a ram pierced the outer layer of stone, the wall crumbled quite easily.

now much larger and were enclosed in a wooden framework like a shed. Protected from stones and fire-arrows by layers of padding and wet hides, they could be wheeled up to the walls. Gangs of soldiers swung the ram back and forth against the wall, safe under cover from the defenders' missiles. Tall siege towers, like moving forts, were pushed against the fortifications, and attackers clambered across from the tower on to the ramparts.

▽ A 4th-century battering ram, covered with brushwood padding and wet rawhide. The metal-headed beam swung on ropes from a strong frame. Sometimes defenders dropped heavy logs to snap off the neck of the beam where it stuck out in front. Sometimes they dangled nooses over the wall to catch the head of the ram and pull the shed over.

▷ Some siege towers were as tall as 115 ft (35 m), with ten floors connected inside by ladders. Light catapults fired through hatches, and archers manned the outside galleries. The barrage of stones and arrows forced the defenders off their ramparts, while attack-parties climbed the ladders under cover. The towers were pushed along on rollers.

The Macedonian conquerors

In 360 BC, as the weakened city-states of Greece continued their endless wrangles, a ruthless, energetic young king took the throne of Macedonia. Philip II built up a superb army and embarked on a series of campaigns against the Greek city-states. He finally defeated them in 338 BC at the Battle of Chaeronea and became master of Greece. Two years later he was succeeded by his son Alexander. Within twelve years Alexander the Great had won an immortal name as one of the world's great conquerors.

The Macedonian army of the 4th century BC was in many ways an improvement over the old phalanx. At the heart of the army was still the armored spearman standing in a massed formation. But this formation was now much stronger and deeper. The Macedonians used a battalion 16 men wide by 16 men deep, which could attack with much greater weight than the old 8-deep phalanx.

Instead of a stabbing spear, which left all but the front two or three ranks of the phalanx out of reach of the fighting, the Macedonians used a huge pike, up to 20 ft 8 in (6.3 m) long. When the soldiers held these pikes out in front of them, the heads of the first five ranks of pikes stuck out beyond the formation in a wicked steel hedge; it was impossible for any enemy with shorter weapons to get near the soldiers.

Another and most important change made by the Macedonians was the introduction of strong cavalry forces. Macedonia was flatter country than southern Greece, and good horses were bred on its plains.

▽ Junior officer of Macedonian pikemen. Plumes and a painted spiral on his helmet show his rank. His bronze, painted armor is shaped like the hoplite's linen cuirass. He needs both hands for his pike, so his shield hangs from a neckstrap, which takes some of the weight off his left arm.

28

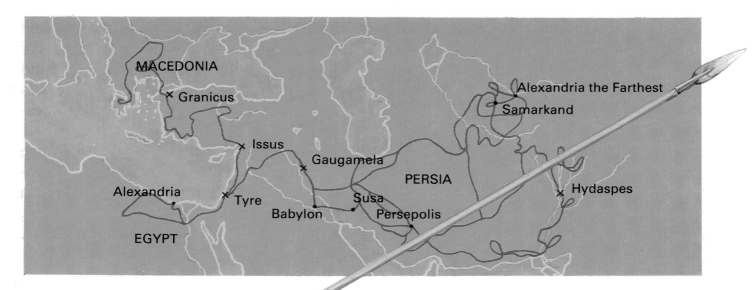

◁ A Thessalian cavalry officer of Alexander's army. His rank is shown by the silver wreath on his helmet and by his panther-skin saddle cloth.

△ Route of Alexander's armies. In just 12 years Alexander conquered the whole Greek world, the Middle East, and western Asia as far as southern Russia and the borders of India. Many of the lessons taught by his success were remembered by the Romans who rose to power in this region 150 years later.

Philip and Alexander raised many regiments of cavalry from the Macedonian noblemen and their ranch-hands.

The riders were armored like infantrymen and armed with long lances. They were trained to ride in disciplined formations and to charge enemy infantry and cavalry on the battlefield, instead of making the hit-and-run attacks usual in those days. Alexander often led his own Companion Cavalry regiment in person at the head of its wedge-shaped formation.

Alexander's army was a balanced mixture of heavy and light infantry and cavalry, many recruited among the Asian peoples he defeated.

Glossary

Boeotia   Region of Greece around the city of Thebes; its flat plains were used for growing grain crops and raising horses.

Cadet   A young soldier under training.

City-state   An independent community in ancient Greece – a large town and its surrounding farmlands. Small towns were usually forced to band together in alliances under the leadership of large, powerful states like Athens and Sparta.

Crete   Island in the eastern Mediterranean, famous in ancient times for its skilled archers.

Cuirass   Armor covering a man's chest and back down to the waist.

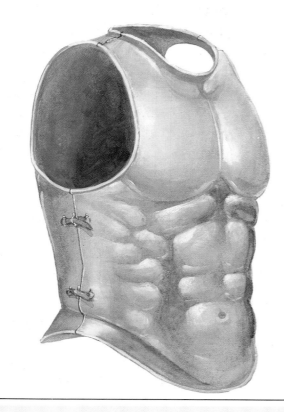

Galley   Long, narrow ship mainly powered by oarsmen sitting on benches all along the sides. Ancient galleys also had a mast and sail, for cruising when the wind was favorable.

Greaves   Curved pieces of armor, shaped like gutters, which protected the shins.

Helot   Slave in Sparta. Helots did all farming and other work, leaving Spartan citizens free for full-time soldiering.

Hoplite   Ancient Greek armored spearman: from the word *hoplon*, a shield.

Javelin   Light spear, used for throwing at the enemy.

Kopis   Type of ancient Greek sword. It had a heavy, slightly curved blade sharpened on one side only, and was used with a chopping stroke.

Metic   Term meaning a non-Athenian free Greek man given permission to settle in Athens. Metics took care of much of the city's trade and commerce, for Athenians were snobbish about making a living by business.

Peltast   A lightly armed, unarmored Greek soldier, so-called from the pelta, a light wickerwork shield which he used. Peltasts were usually either foreign mercenaries, or citizens too poor to afford a hoplite's armor.

Phalanx The massed formation of armored spearmen used by all ancient Greek armies.

Rhodes Island in the southeast Aegean Sea, famous in ancient times for its skilled slingers.

Scythians Nomadic people who lived in ancient times on the plains north of the Black Sea; they were famous for their skill as horsemen and bowmen.

Slave A person legally owned by another; a life-long bond-servant, without individual rights. Slavery was known throughout the ancient world, and all ancient economies were based upon it.

Slingers Men who used slings for hunting or fighting. A stone, or a specially made bullet of clay or metal, was whirled round the head in a leather pocket on two strings, then released at high speed. Ancient slingers were so accurate that they were said to be able to hit a charging bull on whichever horn they aimed at. Sling-stones killed at hundreds of yards' range, and could even crush a metal helmet.

Thessaly Region in the far north of Greece, where horses were bred in ancient times.

Thrace Region now known as Bulgaria; in ancient times, a wild frontier area inhabited by fierce hill tribes, who often hired out as mercenaries.

498 BC Greek colonies in Asia Minor rebel unsuccessfully against Darius, king of Persia, helped by Greek mainland states.

490 BC Darius invades Greece; Persians defeated by Athenians at Marathon.

480 BC Darius's son Xerxes invades Greece once more. Spartan force, under Leonidas, wiped out at Thermopylae after heroic resistance. Athenian and allied navies destroy Persian fleet off Salamis.

479 BC Greek victories over Persians at Plataea and Mycale end Persian threat.

478 BC Athens forms Delian League, leading alliance of 100 states in rivalry to Sparta's Peloponnesian League. For the next 70 years, constant unrest and occasional open warfare between shifting Athenian and Spartan alliances.

457 BC Pericles of Athens completes fortification of Athens and its port, Piraeus.

418 BC Sparta defeats several rebellious ex-allies at 1st Battle of Mantinea.

414 BC Disastrous defeat of Athenian army at Syracuse in Sicily.

406 BC Athenian fleet destroyed by Spartans at Aegospotami. Athens besieged, and surrenders. Sparta now overlord of Greece.

394 BC Sparta defeats rebellious Athens, Thebes and Corinth.

371 BC Epaminondas of Thebes defeats Spartans at Leuctra. A short period of Theban domination follows.

354 BC King Philip II of Macedon begins his campaigns of expansion.

338 BC Philip defeats Athens and Thebes at Chaeronea, and becomes overlord of Greece.

336 BC Philip assassinated; Alexander the Great comes to throne of Macedon and leadership of Greek world.

Index

Aegean Sea 4, 5, 31
Aegospotami, Battle of 31
Alexander the Great 28, 29, 31
Alexandria 29
archers 20, 24, 30
armor 4, 10, 12–13, 20, 28, 29, 30
arrows 14, 20, 26, 27
Athens 4, 5, 6, 7, 10, 24, 25, 30, 31
athletics 8

Babylon 29
barracks 10, 22, 23
baths 8, 22
battalion 28
battering ram 26, 27
battle 10, 12, 13, 14, 16, 17, 18, 19, 23, 24, 25, 29
Black Sea 20, 31
Boeotia 20, 30
boxing 8

cadet 7, 10, 30
catapult 26, 27
cavalry 20, 28, 29
Chaeronea, Battle of 28, 31
citizenship 6, 7, 22, 24
city assembly 6
city-state 4, 5, 22, 28, 30
cloaks 20, 22
company 14
Corinth 5, 12, 31
Crete 5, 20, 30
cuirass 12, 13, 28, 30

dagger 29
Darius 31
Delian League 31
discus 8

education 8, 22
Egypt 29
Epaminondas 31

farming 4, 6, 22
fire-arrows 26, 27
food 10, 22
fortress 10, 26

galleys 24–5, 30
Gaugamela 29
grain 6, 30
Granicus 29
grapes 6
greaves 4, 13, 16, 30

helmet 4, 12, 16, 28, 29
helot 22, 30
hoplon 30
horse-archers 20
horses 7, 20, 28, 30, 31
Hydaspes 29

India 29
Issus 29

javelin 8, 20, 30

kopis 13, 30

lances 29
Leonidas 31
Leuctra, Battle of 17, 31

Macedonia 5, 28, 29, 31
Mantinea, Battle of 31
Marathon, Battle of 31
medical attention 10
mercenaries 20, 31
metics 6, 7, 30
military training 4, 10–11, 22
Mycale, Battle of 31

navies 25, 31

oarsmen 24–5, 30
olives 6, 10

Peloponnesian League 31
pelta 20, 30
peltasts 20, 30
pension 10
Pericles 31
Persepolis 29
Persia 25, 29, 31
phalanx 14, 16, 19, 20, 28, 31
Philip II of Macedon 28, 29, 31
pike 28

Piraeus 31
Plataea, Battle of 31
platoon 14

rations 22
Rhodes 5, 20, 31
Romans 29
Russia 29

sailors 24
Salamis, Battle of 25, 31
Samarkand 29
Scythia 20, 31
shield 10, 11, 13, 14, 16, 20, 23, 28
ships 24–5
Sicily 31
siege machines 26–7
siege tower 27
slaves 6, 7, 8, 22, 24, 31
slings 20, 31
Sparta 4, 5, 17, 22–3, 30, 31
spear 4, 10, 13, 14, 16, 20, 28, 30
Susa 29
sword 13, 30
Syracuse 31

Thebes 5, 17, 31
Thermopylae 31
Thessaly 5, 20, 29, 31
Thrace 5, 12, 20, 31
trade 6, 24, 30
tunics 10, 20, 22
Tyre 29

veterans 7, 10, 14
voting 6, 10, 22

warships 24–5
weapons 4, 8, 10, 13, 20, 28
wine 6
wrestling 8

Xerxes 31

PRINTED IN BELGIUM BY
proost
INTERNATIONAL BOOK PRODUCTION

Edward S. Curtis
Portraits

The Many Faces Of The Native American

Wayne L. Youngblood

CHARTWELL
BOOKS

Brimming with creative inspiration, how-to projects, and useful information to enrich your everyday life, Quarto Knows is a favorite destination for those pursuing their interests and passions. Visit our site and dig deeper with our books into your area of interest: Quarto Creates, Quarto Cooks, Quarto Homes, Quarto Lives, Quarto Drives, Quarto Explores, Quarto Gifts, or Quarto Kids.

Inspiring | Educating | Creating | Entertaining

This edition published in 2017 by Chartwell Books
an imprint of The Quarto Group
142 West 36th Street, 4th Floor
New York, NY 10018 USA

ISBN: 978-0-7858-3559-2

Printed and bound in China

10 9 8 7 6 5 4 3 2 1

Designer: Mark Tennent

Page 1: This pair of grinning Nunivak boys pose in a kaiak (kayak). They were taught all the skills they'd need from an early age and were honored with feasts when they took their first game, c.1929.
Published in *The North American Indian*, Supplement to Volume XX.
Library of Congress, Prints & Photographs Division, Edward S. Curtis Collection, LC-USZ62-46892

Page 2: Agichida, Assiniboin (XVIII portfolio) This Assiniboin, with a blanket over his denim shirt, exhibits strong Indian features that Curtis felt were characteristic of the type.
Library of Congress, Prints & Photographs Division, Edward S. Curtis Collection, LC-USZ62-136608

Right: Shiwawatiwa, a Zuni Indian
Library of Congress, Prints & Photographs Division, Edward S. Curtis Collection, LC-USZ62-111133

MIX
Paper from responsible sources
FSC® C016973
www.fsc.org

CONTENTS

Introduction		6
I	The Apache. The Jicarillas. The Navaho.	23
II	The Pima. The Papago. The Qahatika. The Mohave. The Yuma. The Maricopa. The Walapai. The Havasupai. The Apache-Mohave, or Yavapai	37
III	The Teton Sioux. The Yanktonai. The Assiniboin.	51
IV	The Apsaroke, or Crows. The Hidatsa.	63
V	The Mandan. The Arikara. The Atsina.	79
VI	The Piegan. The Cheyenne. The Arapaho.	91
VII	The Yakima. The Klickitat. The Salishan tribes of the interior. The Kutenai.	107
VIII	The Nez Perces. Wallawalla. The Umatilla. The Cayuse. The Chinookan tribes.	121
IX	The Salishan tribes of the coast. The Chimakum and the Quilliute. The Willapa.	133
X	The Kwakiutl.	143
XI	The Nootka. The Haida.	153
XII	The Hopi.	159
XIII	The Hupa. The Yurok. The Karok. The Wiyot. The Tolowa and Tututni. The Shasta. The Achomawi. The Klamath.	169
XIV	The Kato. The Wailaki. The Yuki. The Pomo. The Wintun. The Maidu. The Miwok. The Yokuts.	183
XV	The Southern California Shoshoneans. The Diegueños. The Plateau Shoshoneans. The Washo.	193
XVI	The Tiwa. The Keres.	201
XVII	The Tewa. The Zuñi.	211
XVIII	The Chipewyan. The Western Woods Cree. The Sarsi.	225
XIX	The Indians of Oklahoma. The Wichita. The Southern Cheyenne. The Oto. The Comanche. The Peyote Cult.	231
XX	The Alaskan Eskimo. The Nunivak. The Eskimo of Hooper Bay. The Eskimo of King Island. The Eskimo of Little Diomede Island. The Eskimo of Cape Prince. The Kotzebue Eskimo. The Noatak. The Kobuk. The Selawik.	239
Index		256

INTRODUCTION

A few of the faces show joy. Others are marked with deep lines of care, worry or the fear of an unknown future. Some even convey annoyance with the photographer. All are highly expressive. Whatever they show—or are perceived to show—the portraits of American Indians made by Edward Sheriff Curtis communicate the full range of emotions inherent in the human condition. Curtis saw time, progress and culture rushing forward, engulfing and crushing the way of life of the American Indian with it. He ended up giving more than 30 years of his life, his financial security, his marriage and even his health to capture what he perceived was the final hurrah of the American Indian. Yet he never started out to complete such an ambitious project. Curtis' first love—and goal—was to be a successful portrait artist—and he was—but as he became increasingly aware of the "vanishing Indian," he felt called to a mission of sorts.

"You and I know, and of course everybody does who thinks of it, the Indians of North America are vanishing. They've crumbled from their pride and power into pitifully small numbers, painful poverty and sorry weakness. There won't be anything left of them in a few generations and it's a tragedy—a national tragedy," Curtis wrote to his friend George Bird Grinnell in 1898.

"Bird—I believe I can do something about it. I have some ability. I can live with these people, get their confidence, understand them and photograph them in all their natural attitudes. I can start—and sell prints of my pictures as I go along. I'm a poor man but I've got my health, plenty of steam and something to work for."

President Theodore Roosevelt, himself no friend of the Indian, noted in his introduction to Volume I of Curtis' 20-volume *The North American Indian*, that "the Indian as he has hitherto been is on the point of passing away." While Roosevelt felt the sooner this happened the better, he at least thought that the so-called "vanishing race" should be documented, and he supported Curtis' efforts wholeheartedly.

As Curtis traveled throughout the Southwest, West, and Northwest during the opening decades of the 20th century, he wasn't alone. Dozens of other photographers possessing various levels of skill roamed the country too, trying either to capture the end of a passing era or to profit from an almost sideshow mentality toward the American Indians and what they represented. The depiction of Indians, their habits and especially their sacred customs was a profitable practice indeed. Fred Harvey and the Detroit Publishing Co. both made fortunes from Indians (and those who photographed them) through the sales of countless popular picture postcards and other curios.

It's rather interesting to note that as well known as Edward S. Curtis and his work have become to people worldwide, few think of him first as a portrait artist. He's considered by most as an artistic photographer of American Indians and their life. Secondarily, he is thought of as an ethnographer and historian. Yet, Curtis as a portraitist should come as no surprise. He cut his teeth on commercial

"The passing of every old man or woman means the passing of some tradition, some knowledge of sacred rites possessed by no other...consequently the information that is to be gathered, for the benefit of future generations, respecting the mode of life of one of the great races of mankind, must be collected at once or the opportunity will be lost for all time." **Edward S. Curtis**

Far Left: An unnamed Qahatika child photographed in 1907 wears a blanket to emphasize her face. Like many Curtis portraits, one gets the feeling of looking at the person, rather than a photo.
Library of Congress, Prints & Photographs Division, Edward S. Curtis Collection, LC-USZC4-8845

Left: "Apache Girl and Papoose." The baby stares at the camera, the mother at the baby. Taken in Curtis' field tent this portrait shows the obvious joy of the mother.
Library of Congress, Prints & Photographs Division, Edward S. Curtis Collection, LC-USZC4-8845

portraiture, successfully operating two studios and later utilizing many of the conventions of classic portraiture in scores of images from his massive 20-volume *The North American Indian*. Many of these captivating images are either formal-looking sittings or were posed in ways that very much call classic portraiture to mind—if one looks closely.

The anatomy of a portrait

Classic portraiture, as considered by most, deals most heavily with faces and expressions, with everything else in the image subservient to those elements. To effectively communicate these facial expressions through classic portraiture, five basic facial views are used: full-front, three-quarters (both left and right) and profile (both left and right). Very rarely does the nose break the linear plane of the cheek, and various upward and downward tilts of the head are used to emphasize features or expressions. The basic five-view philosophy applies equally to facial, three-quarters or full-length portraits. Your eyes should be drawn immediately to the face and expression and what they are communicating.

The skilled portrait artist also serves as a form of facial editor. In commercial photography a photographer first studies a client's face, then relies on lighting and facial angle to select and enhance

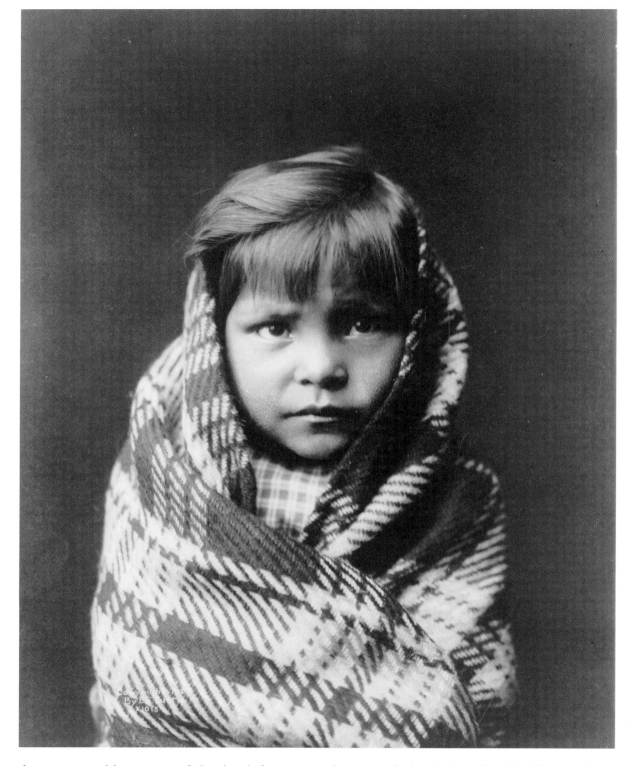

those most positive aspects of the sitter's features,
while downplaying potentially unflattering aspects.

In addition to the facial views, tilt and lighting,
there is a principle used primarily for portrait
composition known as the Golden Mean (related to
the rule of thirds). Thought to originate with the
ancient Greeks, the Golden Mean represents the
point where the center of focal interest should lie.
To find the Golden Mean, draw a diagonal line
connecting two diagonal corners. Next, draw lines
from the remaining corners so they meet the first
diagonal at a perpendicular angle. Important

elements of the design should fall near these
intersections. If you were to examine Curtis' portrait
works in this manner, you would find the vast
majority of his portraits are textbook examples of
classical portraiture. He was a master of technique.

Of course, any form of meaningful portraiture,
however—photographic or otherwise—is the
direct result of communication between the artist
and the subject. This is why even some abstract
portraits and caricatures are effective depictions of
their subjects. Technical proficiency is not an end
in itself. It serves only as a vehicle of the portrait by

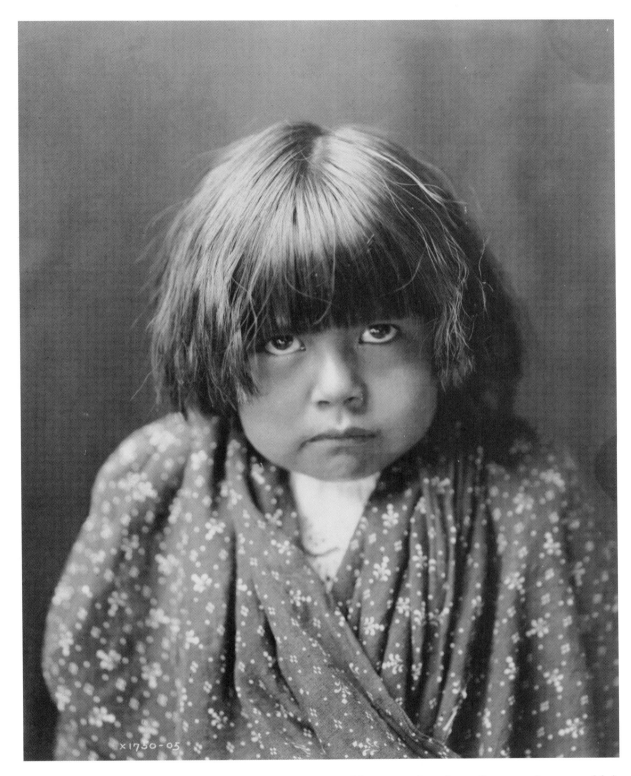

establishing pose, lighting, facial tilt and camera position to reflect those aspects of a subject's face an artist wishes to highlight. Technique, therefore, is the language used by a portrait artist for communicating his artistic statement as expressed by the subject.

One of the things that set Curtis so far apart from his contemporaries was his equal—if not occasionally greater—concern for the art form over simple documentation. Curtis consistently paid very close attention to setting (natural or posed), lighting, props, potential reproduction problems and other factors that wouldn't necessarily bother the snapshot artist or traveling photographer for hire. Ironically, these also are all the things that brought eventual criticism his way as an ethnographer. By paying such close attention to detail, Curtis frequently changed or embellished settings, garments or props to serve his artistic eye. This led skeptics to accuse Curtis—at best—of muddying the ethnological waters, and—at worst—outright fakery. But Curtis was first and foremost an artist, the result of many years of perfecting his chosen craft.

Right: Ah Chee Lo, photographed by Curtis in 1905, stares directly into the camera with a somewhat piercing gaze. *Library of Congress, Prints & Photographs Division, Edward S. Curtis Collection, LC-USZ62-106987*

Far Right: Although not a portrait in the traditional sense, "The Drink," from 1905, shows how Curtis left nothing to chance when setting up a shot—even outdoors. *Library of Congress, Prints & Photographs Division, Edward S. Curtis Collection, LC-USZ62-123300*

A growing interest

Curtis first became interested in photography and the outdoors as a boy growing up in Minnesota. He was born near Whitewater, Wis., in 1868, the second child of Johnson Asahel Curtis and Ellen Sheriff Curtis. Curtis moved with his family to Minnesota when he was five. His father, who served in the Union Army during the Civil War and had very fragile health as a result, had a difficult time supporting his family. He tried

subsistence farming and, later, a grocery store, but with little success. As his grocery business was winding down, Johnson Curtis became an evangelical preacher and traveled a great deal to visit his parishioners. Curtis accompanied his father on many of these trips through the inland waterways of Minnesota to remote areas, camping, cooking, paddling and toting heavy bags. He developed a deep love of the outdoors and the tasks associated with surviving in the wild—skills

Right: In this 1905 head-and-shoulders portrait of a Yaqui matron, Curtis made no effort to hide her modern cloths, but again emphasizes her face with a head covering. *Library of Congress, Prints & Photographs Division, Edward S. Curtis Collection, LC-USZ62-104493*

that would be essential to him later, as he documented Western Indian tribes.

Ironically, Curtis recalled later in life that the first book he remembered reading was a bloody account of the Sioux Indian uprising of 1862, which occurred just a few miles from what became the Curtis home. During the uprising several hundred White settlers were killed, and thousands more were driven from their homes. Despite being

White, Curtis developed an early sympathy for Indians, and understood that the Sioux had been pushed beyond their breaking point. They had been driven from their ancestral lands, Christian missionaries were interfering with their native beliefs, White settlers were killing and scaring the wild game away, and the government broke promise after promise, completely destroying its credibility with the Indians. As he traveled and

camped with his father, Curtis tried to envision all the horrors that had taken place on those lands just 20 or so years before. "The immediate outcome of this deplorable affair," Curtis wrote, "was a nation-wide cry for the total elimination of all American Indians. Radicals even suggested that small pox germs be implanted among all tribes, giving no thought to how this scourge would be contained." But this wasn't necessary, as disease was already ravaging the Indian population, and thousands more were killed by whites from then until the end of the century. Curtis, of course, would have heard contemporaneously of the hundreds of battles taking place with Indians throughout the West, culminating with the Wounded Knee massacre in 1890, when somewhere between 150 and 300 mostly unarmed men, women and children were killed by American soldiers.

Right: Head-and-shoulders portrait of an Acoma woman. The print fabric and squash-blossom necklace she is wearing emphasize her impassive expression; c.1905.
Library of Congress, Prints & Photographs Division, Edward S. Curtis Collection, LC-USZC4-8853

Far Right: "Moki Melon Eaters." Curtis took several photos of these little girls. This particular shot (with added lines) illustrates the Golden Mean. (Volume XII)
Library of Congress, Prints & Photographs Division, Edward S. Curtis Collection, LC-USZ62-112226

When he was 12, Curtis built his first camera, using a stereopticon lens his father brought home from the war, mounting it on a double-box frame, according to instructions found in *Wilson's Photographics: A Series of Lessons Accompanied by Notes on All Processes Which are Needful in Photography*, an 1881 guide to the relatively young art of photography. The guide gave information ranging from the construction of a rough camera, to equipment care and composition, as well as printing. He continued to develop his skills and took an apprentice position with a photography shop in St. Paul when he was 17.

During the fall of 1887, Curtis accompanied his now frail father out West, where they homesteaded near what is now Port Orchard, Wash. He continued to work on his photographic skills and took an interest in the local Indians, who

were quite different from those who had lived in Minnesota. A year later, his mother and siblings came to Washington to join Edward and his father, but his father died a few days after they arrived. Edward now had the full burden of supporting his family, and any dreams he had of becoming a photographer were shelved for the time being.

In 1890, however, Curtis fell and was injured while working in a lumberyard. He was no longer able to do the hard labor he had been doing. He bought a large-view camera (14 by 17 inches) from a gold miner and began taking scenic photographs of the area. He preferred the high-quality images formed by glass-plate negatives over those created by cheaper "hundred-shot" film used by amateur shutterbugs of the day. His mother was concerned about Curtis' waste of time and money, but he was now serious about his art and his plans to become a professional. In 1891, he sold the family's largely unprofitable brickyard, mortgaged the family homestead and bought a partnership in a downtown Seattle photography shop for $150. The partners,

Left: A formal studio pose by Heyn & Matzen in 1900 shows a Sioux mother with her child. While sympathetic, it does not convey the same level of communication found with Curtis' subjects. *Library of Congress, Prints & Photographs Division, LC-USZ62-95143*

The Orotone process

"The ordinary photographic print, however good, lacks depth and transparency, or more strictly speaking, translucency. We all know how beautiful are the stones and pebbles in the limpid brook of the forest where the water absorbs the blue of the sky and the green of the foliage, yet when we take the same iridescent pebbles from the water and dry them they are dull and lifeless, so it is with the ordinary photographic print, but in the Curt-Tones all the transparency is retained and they are as full of life and sparkle as an opal."

Edward S. Curtis, from advertising material

The goldtone, or orotone, photographic process was not created by Curtis, but he worked on, improved and refined the technique until his name became synonymous with it. Curtis even named these images after himself, calling them "Curt-Tones," and vintage Curt-Tones in their original frames are among the most prized Curtis images.

Similar to its older cousin, the ambrotype (which was patented in 1854), a goldtone, simply put, is a positive image on glass, rather than printed on paper. To create a goldtone (as a simplified explanation), Curtis first took a plate of glass and spread emulsion onto the surface. He then exposed the plate to one of his negatives (by projecting it on the surface), exposing and fixing the wet emulsion-covered glass and creating a positive image. Like the ambrotype, goldtone photos require some form of backing to help reflect the silver present in the emulsion. Because glass is transparent, it does not reflect highlights and shadows on subjects in both ambrotypes and goldtone photos, making them difficult to see. Unlike the ambrotype, however, the goldtone was not one-of-a-kind (because of Curtis' use of projected negatives rather than shooting directly to plate), and the backing was a gold color, rather than a black lacquer. For the backing material Curtis mixed a combination of banana oils and bronzing powers to create the desired color. He then spread this mixture over the emulsion (image) side of the glass plate. The net result was stunning. Curtis' goldtone portraits in particular take on a luminescent quality, with light reflecting off the gold backing, highlighting details of the subjects' faces and garments, giving a light-filled three-dimensional effect. The final step in Curtis' process—and one integral to his marketing—involved backing the glass image, framing and sealing it. This not only protected the work, but gave Curtis a unique type of product.

Curtis and Rasmus Rothi, renamed the business "Rothi & Curtis, Photographers," but the partnership lasted less than a year. In 1892, shortly after he married, Curtis formed a new partnership with Thomas Guptil (sometimes spelled Gupthill), and within a few years the business was thriving. Both men soon developed a high reputation for the fine quality of their portraits, and most of Seattle's high society would not consider going elsewhere for their photographic needs. By 1896, Curtis and Guptil were considered the finest photographers in Seattle, and *Argus* magazine reported on a particular type of photography in which the two young men excelled—photographs on a "gold or silver plaque," which was described as "brilliant and beautiful beyond description." These were examples of silvertone and orotone processes on glass, and Curtis later made the orotone, or "Curt-Tone," as he preferred to call it, his hallmark. Curtis became sole owner of the portrait studio business in 1897, and the reputation of Edward S. Curtis, Photographer and Photoengraver, continued to grow.

Photography as a means of conveying emotion

Curtis' career as a rapidly rising portrait artist (and, ultimately, the first half of his *North American Indian* project) coincided with the growing movement known as Pictorialism in the United States. Pictorialism describes the artistic use of the camera as opposed to its purely documentary function, to the extent that images created were at the very least posed to emulate paintings and other forms of art. In other cases images were manipulated in the darkroom to create unusual effects. The ultimate goal, through use of these numerous techniques, was to enhance the emotional impact of a photo far beyond what the shutter "saw." Curtis' work appeared regularly in important camera journals of the period, including *Camera Craft*, the West Coast's leading photography publication.

In some ways it's a bit ironic that Curtis was honing his photographic skills during a time when photography and its merits were being contested hotly. Artists and society alike still weren't exactly sure whether photography had a valid role in the arts. In some circles photography was considered almost a form of cheating, because artists were beginning to use photos as sources for other artistic renderings, rather than working from life. The introduction of the Kodak #1 snapshot camera in 1888 (a simple box camera with a 100-exposure roll of film) didn't help the argument that photography was art. These gadgets turned thousands of people into camera fiends, few with any technical or artistic skill. When the entire roll had been exposed, the intact camera was sent to the factory, where it was reloaded and returned while the first roll was being processed. This cheapening of the photographic process made Curtis and others like him veer towards truly fine photography and techniques that reinforced the camera's product as an art, including effects such as platinum and silver prints, orotones and hand-colored prints.

In 1902, as part of the Pictorialism movement, Alfred Stieglitz founded the Photo Secession movement, which was dedicated to establishing photography as an art, rather than as simply either a documentary tool or a pastime. While Curtis wasn't a part of the group, his philosophy was similar. He believed that good photography was the product of study, not chance. As a result, even before beginning to photograph Indians, he carefully posed his subjects, worked with the light and backgrounds, and utilized techniques that diffused light, blurred backgrounds and softened edges. He also touched up photographs for effect. In part, this is what earned him his reputation as the top portrait photographer in Seattle.

But it's also his philosophy towards quality art photography and the techniques he used that has allowed him to be discounted in the eyes of some ethnographers and armchair anthropologists, for obvious reasons.

Rediscovering Indians

Meanwhile, back in the studio, Curtis' touch on a portrait was as good as gold. His reputation continued to spread, and he didn't have to look for work.

In ventures away from the portrait studio, Curtis began to explore the waters and mountains of Puget Sound and spent a great deal of time in the outdoors with his camera. In 1895, he also began photographing an aged Indian woman, "Princess Angeline," as she was known to area residents. She was Kickisomlo, the Suquamish daughter of Chief Seattle (Sealth), for whom the city was named.

"The first photograph I ever made of Indians was of Princess Angeline, the digger and dealer in clams," Curtis wrote. *"I paid the princess a dollar for each picture I made. This seemed to please her greatly and with hands and jargon she indicated that she preferred to spend her time having her picture taken than digging for clams."*

In 1898, Curtis won awards from the National Photographic Society for images of Princess Angeline and other Indians.

As an amateur mountain climber Curtis was about to meet an individual who would change the entire course of his life. Late one afternoon in 1898, Curtis was pitching his tent at Camp Muir and saw a group of men approaching the Nisqually Glacier. He knew they were completely unaware of the extreme danger to which they were exposing themselves and offered to bring them back to his camp for the evening. The men were part of a scientific party that included George Bird Grinnell, editor of *Forest and Stream* magazine and naturalist; Clinton Hart Merriam, a

Above: A portrait of the daughter of Chief Siahl—Seattle—Princess Angeline. Angeline was the first Indian Curtis photographed. He took several portraits and action shots in 1895. *Corbis*

Above: Many photographers of Indians posed them in full regalia with modern gadgets in unflattering ways. Images such as this 1916 example by Frank Palmer made popular postcards.
Library of Congress, Prints & Photographs Division, LC-USZ62-101166

Right: Although Alexander Gardner (1821–82) was a talented photographer, his portraits of Indians, such as this portrait of Luig Moraque, a Pima, were stiff.
Library of Congress, Prints & Photographs Division, LC-USZ62-126404

founder of the National Geographic Society and head of the U.S. Biological Survey; and Gifford Pinchot, chief of the U.S. Forest Service. After visiting Curtis in Seattle, the men were so impressed with his work they invited him along as official photographer on a planned expedition to Alaska, funded by railroad tycoon Edward Henry Harriman. The Harriman Expedition became Curtis' opportunity to be exposed to and learn scientific methodology, as well as to begin familiarizing himself with yet more culturally different forms of North American Indians.

That same year, three of Curtis' photos were chosen for a special exhibit of the National Photographic Society. One, called "Homeward," a sunset scene of Indians paddling to shore in a dugout, captured the grand prize and a gold medal, further cementing Curtis' reputation in the young world of photography.

In 1900, Curtis accompanied his friend Grinnell to the northern plains of Montana, for what would become the final great Sun Dance. It was this rite that captured Curtis' imagination and led him on his 30-year quest to document the "old ways" photographically, before it was too late. Curtis specifically chose to document trans-

After leaving Brady's employ, Gardner was commissioned to photograph Indians who came to Washington, D.C., to discuss treaties. These photos, however, almost more resemble mug shots than portraits. O'Sullivan eventually joined Garner's studio as well, and later (1867–69) became official photographer for the U.S. Geological Exploration of the 40th Parallel. His job was to photograph the West in a way that would attract settlers, including a few Indian portraits. Although both men were instrumental in later efforts to document the Indian, their strengths were more attuned to landscape photography or scenes that evoked action. Other early photographers who took portraits of Indians include Louis Heller, William S. Soule, Ben Wittick, Charles Milton Bell, C.L. Hamilton, David F. Barry, and William Henry Jackson, all of whom operated during the 1860s–80s. Most of their work with Indians, however seems rather perfunctory or uninspired, showing little of the personalities of those at whom they aimed their lenses. Jackson (1843–1942) was arguably the most technically skilled of these, using glass plates and the wet collodian method to render usually very high-resolution images of all he shot.

Of those photographers who photographed Indians, it is amazing how many crossed paths. For

Left: A very formal studio portrait of this Yuma Musician (ca. 1870–1912) by Isaiah Taber shows a lackluster "brave" on a stump in full paint, along with playing cards (his vice?). *Library of Congress, Prints & Photographs Division, LC-DIG-ppmsca-08116*

Below: Frank Rinehart was one of the first photographers to create emotional and non-demeaning portraits of Indians. This portrait of a Wichita woman and child is very moving. *Library of Congress, Prints & Photographs Division, LC-DIG-ppmsca-15855*

Mississippi Indian tribes because many of them still maintained at least some of their tradition and culture. Most of the Eastern tribes had been pretty well destroyed and assimilated already.

Within a few weeks of witnessing the Sun Dance, Curtis was on his way to the Southwest (Arizona) to capture the Hopi Snake Dance on film and begin planning his North American Indian project, which he thought would take only 5 years to complete. His path was set.

Other views through a troubled lens

As previously mentioned, Curtis was far from being the only photographer tramping through Indian villages and around reservations during the twilight of the 19th century and dawn of the 20th, as traditional Indian culture was winding down. Numerous others—each with a reason, but none with the same resolve as Curtis—were also shooting natives and native life, as well as the West in general.

Two of the most well-known and earliest of the western photographers (or at least those who photographed Indians) are Timothy O'Sullivan (1840–82) and Alexander Gardner (1821–82), both of whom honed their art under Mathew Brady during the Civil War.

Right: Shout At—
Sioux. Adolf Muhr, who
became Curtis' studio
manager, took more than
1,000 Indian portraits
during the 1898 Tans-
Mississippi Exposition
while employed by
Frank Rinehart.
*Library of Congress, Prints
& Photographs Division,
LC-USZC2-6294*

example, Frank Albert Rinehart (1861–1928)—who also was part Indian—trained under artist-photographer William Henry Jackson. Rinehart established a successful business in Omaha, Neb., where he was eventually commissioned as official photographer of the Indian leaders who attended the Indian Congress in conjunction with the 1898 Trans-Mississippi International Exposition. One of Rinehart's assistants, Adolf Muhr, took more than 1,000 individual studio portraits of Plains Indians during the exposition and the two traveled to Indian reservations for the next two years, photographing Indians and Indian life as they saw it. Their work is considered to be among the most groundbreaking, in terms of depicting Indians in a manner other than as a cold, detached ethnographic study. Rinehart saw the Indians as people, and, much like Curtis, was effective at gaining their trust and showing aspects of their personalities and emotions. Shortly after Rinehart and Muhr finished their reservation tour, Muhr went on to become Curtis' studio manager and chief printer until his death in 1913. Curtis considered him "a genius in the darkroom."

Other photographers (not always well-known) who either began to depict the Indian in a different light or had strong technical skills include Isaiah Taber (1829–1912), Darius Kinsey (1869–1945), J.A. Anderson, Benjamin A. Gifford (1859–1956), Kolb Brothers, Heyn & Matzen, Frank Fiske (1883–1952), Joseph Dixon and Frederick Monson (1865–1929).

Some, like Fiske, specialized in the more formal, studio-type approach to their Indian portraiture. Others, such and Frederick Monson, used a more candid approach.

Karl Moon (1879–1948), however, is perhaps the photographer who has more in common with Curtis than any other. Carl Everton Moon (he spelled his name with a "K" later in life) was born Oct. 5, 1879, in Wilmington, Ohio. Like Curtis, he developed an interest in and sympathy for the Indian at an early age. He learned the art of photography while serving with the National Guard and decided to turn it into his profession after serving 6 years. He began by opening a studio in Albuquerque, N.M., and doing photographic studies of the numerous pueblo Indians in the area. He eventually was placed in charge of the Fred Harvey operations in Grand Canyon, Ariz. Harvey had established a highly successful string of hotels, restaurants and souvenir shops throughout the West and Southwest, mostly along the railroads. Moon moved to California in 1914 and began studying the American Indian much more earnestly, frequently traveling and living with tribes for extended periods of time, while getting to know them and photographing their lifestyle. Like Curtis, Moon believed his studies were science, but the art of photography was at least as important to him, and he worked hard to master his skills. He also had a way of communicating with his

Right: Frank Fiske, a
contemporary of Curtis,
tended to take very stiff
and formal portraits,
such as this image of
No Heart, from 1906.
*Library of Congress, Prints
& Photographs Division,
LC-USZ62-107606*

about 220 subscriptions were ever sold. In 1935, the assets of the project were sold to the Charles Lauriat Company of Boston. Included were 19 additional sets, almost 285,000 prints and the copper gravure plates for many images. Lauriat, a survivor of the 1915 sinking of the *Lusitania*, died in 1937, just two years after acquiring the Curtis material, which then lay forgotten for the next four deacades.

Sometime around 1970, Karl Kernberger of Santa Fe, N.M., rediscovered the Curtis material in the original Boston Lauriat bookstore, and purchased it (along with two other partners, Jack Loeffler and David Padwa). The trio soon launched exhibits at the Pierpoint Morgan Library and the Philadelphia Museum of Art. During the latter part of the 1970s, the group was bought out by an investment group headed by Mark Zaplin (also of Santa Fe), which held the material until 1982, when it was sold to Kenneth Zerbe. Today, Zerbe and his partner, Steven Kern, occasionally sell prints and even some of the original gravure copper printing plates through a gallery.

Since the rediscovery of Curtis through his

Left: Karl Werntz, artist and educator, shot this somewhat haunting amateur portrait in 1902 of Woopa, a Moqui Indian of the Hopi tribe in modern garb. *Library of Congress, Prints & Photographs Division, LC-USZ62-104559*

Below: Karl Moon had much in common with Curtis. His "Little Maid of the Desert" (1914), set against a neutral background, calls Curtis' approach to mind. *Library of Congress, Prints & Photographs Division, LC-USZ6-1918*

subjects, befriending many and reaping the reward of highly expressionistic portraits.

Unlike Curtis, however, Moon found commercial success, not only through his artistic vision (and hand-colored pen-and-ink-highlighted prints known as Lytrit portraits), but also through his vision that photography could be a very powerful tool in advertising. Thus, Moon was able to sell his portraits for commercial use in ads and logos to dozens of companies, including Harvey, Stetson Hats, Seneca Coal Mining, Wells Fargo and many others.

Rediscovering Curtis

After completing the *North American Indian* project with the release of Volume XX in 1930, Curtis suffered a near-complete physical and emotional breakdown. He took only a handful of photos during the rest of his life, and he died in relative obscurity in 1952. A 76-word obituary in the *New York Times* mentioned that he was an authority on Indian history, and that he had been a photographer.

As celebrated as Curtis' efforts were in the early years of his project, the final volume came with virtually no fanfare and attracted very little attention. For years, Curtis had attempted to sell subscriptions to the lavishly produced set, but at a price ranging between $3,000 when they were first offered, and close to $4,500 by completion, only

Above: Frederick Monsen and Curtis almost certainly bumped into each other in the field. This 1908 image of two Hopi children is reminiscent of Curtis' "Moki Melon Eaters" for gentle humor.
Library of Congress, Prints & Photographs Division, LC-USZ62-101159

work in the 1970s, he has been both revered and reviled both as an artist and as an anthropological photographer, depending upon how one views the ethnologicial implications of his work. Most who encounter Curtis' work lie firmly in one camp or the other. It is fact that Curtis manipulated images and settings to better idealize and communicate his idea of the "vanishing race." He also is known to have occasionally used the same garments on members of different tribes, as well as using a few props repeatedly.

As mentioned earlier, some who dislike the practice have accused Curtis of outright fakery, bending reality to fit his idea of something that never existed culturally. Those who believe in Curtis' work are willing to overlook some of the minor infractions in favor of looking at the overall importance of the body of his work. Either way, our modern-day understanding of the many different tribes of American Indians would be far less complete without the sheer breadth and scope of Curtis' work, which can be criticized but not discounted. Indeed, Curtis' photographs and recordings have shaped our vision of North American Indian culture as it existed at the turn of the century more than that of any other individual, or perhaps more than all others combined. Without its vividly tactile evidence, our idea of the early 20th-century Indian would be little more than an idealized notion that changes with the wind. Curtis may have imposed some of his own ideals, but he didn't invent what he saw. The Indian as a race may not have been on the verge of extinction, but the culture was, and Curtis was genuine in his desire to accurately document it as he saw it—and as he knew it had existed even a few short years before. Oddly, Curtis' use of various props (including some that were not traditional) in his durable images has influenced the modern-day "traditional" Indian dress of several tribes—often without the participants knowing this.

The camera by its nature is an imposition to all the Indians Curtis photographed and it can be argued that it changed reality a bit by its very presence. The "Shadowcatcher," as Curtis was known to many Indians, first had to gain their trust, then set up those shots he wanted or needed. Very little could be allowed to chance or to candid shots, and Curtis rarely failed to gain the trust of Indians from any of the more than 80 tribes he photographed.

Curtis did not document American Indians as he found them. He did idealize them and attempted in some cases to create a mystique surrounding them. But he also had a deep and abiding respect for American Indians and carefully avoided demeaning his subjects in any way or inviting any form of ridicule of them. It is a fact that Curtis wished to truly understand the North American Indian and strove to treat his subjects with the respect he felt they deserved. He treated both his subjects and his art very seriously, and did not compromise either.

A century later, the Curtis legacy lives on through his works—not only the images of daily life of Indians from many tribes—but the exquisite portraiture that illuminates the faces of a time now far away.

Volume I

VOLUME I

THE APACHE.
THE JICARILLAS. THE NAVAHO.

Just weeks after witnessing the Sun Dance in Montana in 1900, Edward S. Curtis was on his way to Arizona to begin in earnest his project of capturing the faces, voices and lifestyles of the North American Indian. For the first tangible piece of his work, Curtis chose tribes that lived in Arizona and New Mexico. He spent more time in the Southwest than anywhere else, and a quarter of his entire work (five volumes) is devoted to tribes of the Southwest. A mix of both old and new field work is found in Volumes II, XII, XVI and XVII. His primary goal in this first trip was to see the Snake Dance on the Hopi reservation, and after reaching Winslow, Ariz., Curtis hired a team to pull his equipment 60 miles across the sandy landscape. One interesting event on this journey was the reaction of Indian children to his inflatable air mattress, which earned him the name "man who sleeps on his breath." Curtis was hardly the first White to visit the area. Regularly advertised trips promising "Indians Galore" brought anthropologists, photographers and all manner of gawkers to the Hopi reservation. Even the Harvard Glee Club had visited the year before Curtis arrived. Still, the pueblo setting was exotic. Curtis likely met Ben Wittick, another Western photographer, who died just three years later of a snake bite from a rattler that was part of a sackful he brought as a gift to the Indians. Other notables, including Charles Lummis, director of the Los Angeles Public Library, and ethnomusicologist Natalie Curtis (no relation) were known to be in the area at the time. He also began to build the foundation for his longtime friendship with the Snake Priest, Sikyaletstiwa. Curtis cajoled, traded and paid to gain access to ritualistic information and a sacred skin, and also paid a group to re-create the nine-day Navajo Yeibechei dance, which he described extensively, causing friction in the tribes. Volume I contains a description by Curtis of his goals for the series and a bit of explanation of his methodology. President Theodore Roosevelt, who was very supportive of Curtis' efforts, wrote the foreword.

Previous Page: Apache Yenin Guy. Curtis' portrait of this bare-chested Apache man emphasizes his rather sad eyes. He is wearing a bandana and two feathers. c.1903.
Library of Congress, Prints & Photographs Division, Edward S. Curtis Collection, LC-USZ62-112202

Above: Tah-Lay, a young Apache, is wearing a blanket and headband to conceal his modern clothing and was likely photographed in Curtis' field tent. c.1903.
Library of Congress, Prints & Photographs Division, Edward S. Curtis Collection, LC-USZC4-8810

Right: Oz Sue. The interest in this man's face for Curtis was no doubt the intensity with which he scans the camera. His gaze is emphasized by the blanket and headband. c.1903.
Library of Congress, Prints & Photographs Division, Edward S. Curtis Collection, LC-USZC4-8804

Above: A portrait of Chideh, an Apache youth with a blanket, shows some of the innocence Curtis wished to capture. He frequently selected either young or very old subjects for characteristic close portraits. c.1903.
Published in *The North American Indian*, Supplement to Volume I.
Library of Congress, Prints & Photographs Division, Edward S. Curtis Collection, LC-USZC4-8846

Right: This half-length young Jicarilla portrait shows her far more formally dressed than normal. The tilt of her head and expression indicate she'd rather be doing something else. c.1905.
Library of Congress, Prints & Photographs Division, Edward S. Curtis Collection, LC-USZ62-112203

X1265-04

Above: This formal portrait of a "Jicarilla cowboy" shows an Apache with far more accessories than he would ever have worn. The hat is likely his, though. c.1905.
Library of Congress, Prints & Photographs Division, Edward S. Curtis Collection, LC-USZ62-112205

Right: "The Blanket Maker." Meant to show more about the activity than the subject, this portrait shows the blanket maker, in a blanket, holding her yarn. c.1904.
Library of Congress, Prints & Photographs Division, Edward S. Curtis Collection, LC-USZ62-120925

Copyright 1909
By E.S. Curtis
X 1011

Copyright 1904
By E.S.Curtis
X 1019

Above: This Navajo woman is wearing a silver squash blossom necklace, hishi necklace, concho belt and pleated skirt to show costume. The blanket draped over her shoulders is the same one worn by the woman on page 29. c.1904.
Library of Congress, Prints & Photographs Division, Edward S. Curtis Collection, LC-USZ62-103498

Right: "A Child of the Desert." A head-and-shoulders portrait of a thoughtful-looking chubby-faced Navajo child conjures visions of "traditional" Indians. The blanket and dark background emphasize her face. c.1904.
Library of Congress, Prints & Photographs Division, Edward S. Curtis Collection, LC-USZ62-101175

Copyright 1904
By E S.Curtis
x 1022

Left: "The Chanter." Curtis sometimes focused on close-in portraits that highlighted facial features and textures. In this portrait of a Navajo Indian wrapped in a blanket, one's eyes are drawn to the faraway look in his eyes and the texture of the blanket and headband. c.1905. *Library of Congress, Prints & Photographs Division, Edward S. Curtis Collection, LC-USZ62-103463*

Above: This older Navajo man is wearing a head-band, looking down. The emphasis is on his overall worn countenance, enhanced by the worn leather strap over his shoulder. c.1905. *Library of Congress, Prints & Photographs Division, Edward S. Curtis Collection, LC-USZ62-56512*

Left: "The Patient." By slightly blurring the background, Curtis was able to focus on the intensity of this man's gaze. The rag head-band and a blanket guide the eye to his facial features. c.1905.
Library of Congress, Prints & Photographs Division, Edward S. Curtis Collection, LC-USZ62-103465

Above: In contrast to "The Patient," this slightly heavier elderly man, called De Gazza, with loose hair appears softer and more gentle. c.1903.
Library of Congress, Prints & Photographs Division, Edward S. Curtis Collection, LC-USZ62-112200

Right: The Jicarilla Apache lived in northern New Mexico. Jicarilla dress and hairstyles were illustrated by this man, who does not have eye contact with the camera so that the focus is on the dress, rather than individual.
Library of Congress, Prints & Photographs Division, Edward S. Curtis Collection, LC-USZ62-106251

Right: Vash gon. The almost mug-shot portrait approach of "Vash gon," showing a brightly lit high-contrast profile (and shadow), features the "Jicarilla type" facial features.
Library of Congress, Prints & Photographs Division, Edward S. Curtis Collection, LC-USZC4-8803

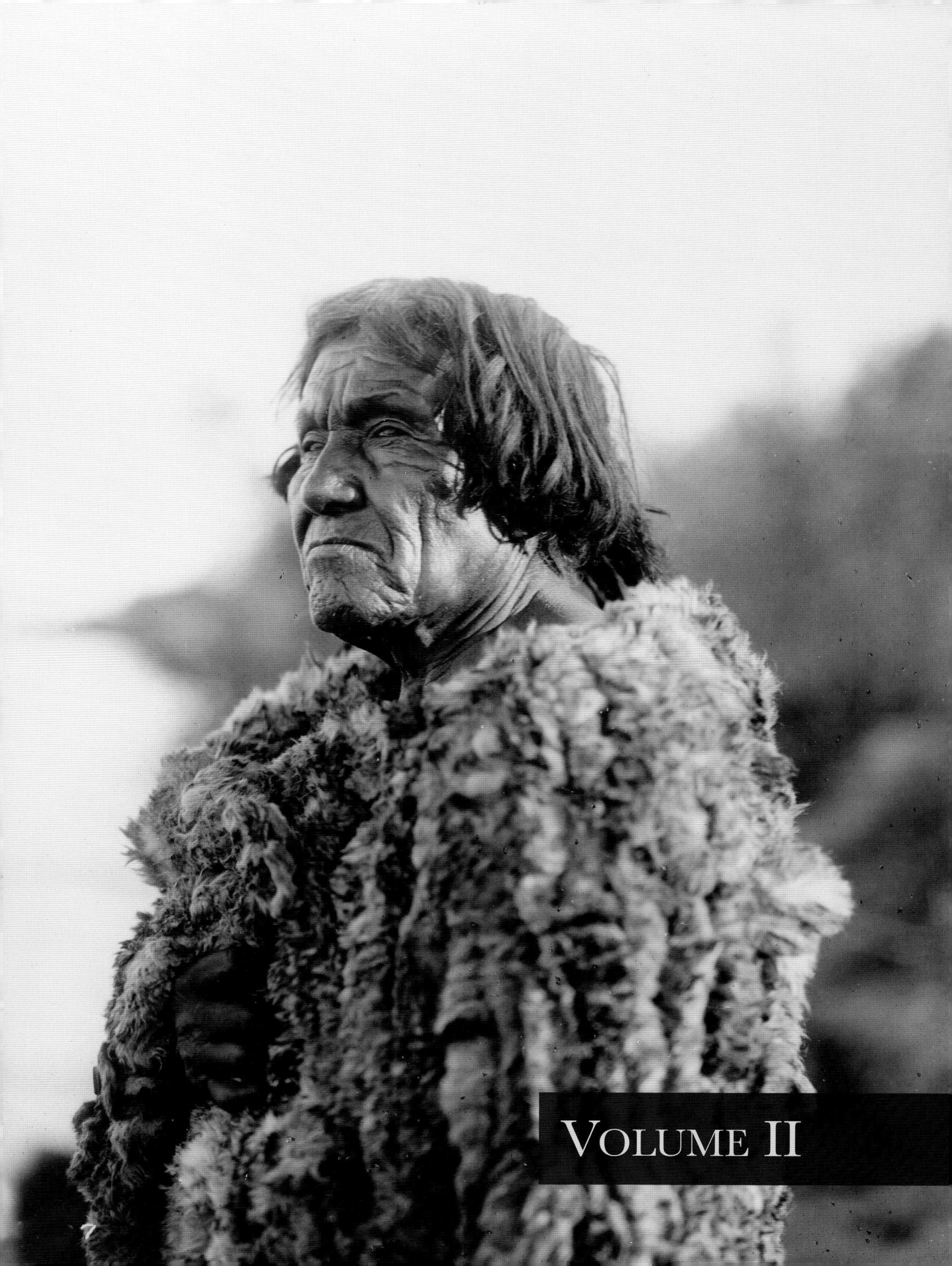

VOLUME II

THE PIMA. THE PAPAGO. THE QAHATIKA. THE MOHAVE. THE YUMA. THE MARICOPA. THE WALAPAI. THE HAVASUPAI. THE APACHE-MOHAVE, OR YAVAPAI.

VOLUME II

PUBLISHED 1908

Staying in the Southwest for Volume II, Curtis grouped nine primarily Arizona tribes (with a bit of Sonora, Mexico, and the edge of southern California). These tribes, related through similar desert lifestyles and two similar languages (Piman and Yuman), were considered very different by Curtis, and he made a great effort to treat each as a culturally distinct group. He elaborated on the various traditions, religious beliefs and rituals of each. Because he had been the subject of a special inquest the year before, regarding the validity of his methodology (which he passed easily), his attention to the scientific method in Volume II was painstaking. Although Curtis had done much of the groundwork for the first three volumes well before there was a concrete plan for publishing the series (most photos were taken between 1900–05), he copyrighted all images in Volume II in 1907. By the time Volume II was released Curtis already was beginning to realize that his original timeline of five years wasn't nearly enough. He also was beginning to realize the cost also was much greater than he anticipated, although he had no way of knowing how deeply in debt he'd eventually become. While doing his field work for the Havasupai, or "Blue Water People," who live at the bottom of Cataract Canyon (a branch of the Grand Canyon), Curtis' camera fell and was smashed. This necessitated 12 hours of laborious repair to piece it together enough to finish the season. He also began his longtime habit of seeking government support for the tribes he studied by intervening on behalf of the Havasupai.

Above: O Che Che, a Mohave photographed by Curtis in 1903, still kept her hair in a traditional manner, but wore a calico dress and print shawl. Mohave women typically wore little more than a knee-length skirt of willow-bark cloth.
Library of Congress, Prints & Photographs Division, Edward S. Curtis Collection, LC-USZ62-109712

Previous Page: Curtis photographed this Mohave man wearing a "primitive" rabbit skin robe in 1907. The rabbit skin robe was no doubt used because it tied in well with the rugged features of the man's face.
Library of Congress, Prints & Photographs Division, Edward S. Curtis Collection, LC-USZ62-101178

Right: Czele Marie (schoolgirl): To focus attention on the facial features of this Pima girl Curtis left her simple print dress and wrapped her hair in a blanket. c.1907.
Library of Congress, Prints & Photographs Division, Edward S. Curtis Collection, LC-USZ62-112212

Left: Qahatika child; c.1907. The Qahatika, once a part of the Pima, lived in five small villages 40 miles from the Pima reservation. Legends suggest that the Qahatika bands escaped into the barren desert after attacks by the Apache and stayed put.
Library of Congress, Prints & Photographs Division, Edward S. Curtis Collection, LC-USZ62-112213

Above: About this portrait of Mosa, Curtis wrote "It would be difficult to conceive of a more aboriginal than this Mohave girl. Her eyes are those of the fawn of the forest, questioning the strange things of civilization upon which it gazes for the first time. She is such a type as Father Garces may have viewed on his journey through the Mohave country in 1776."
Library of Congress, Prints & Photographs Division, Edward S. Curtis Collection LC-USZC4-8920

Above: Mat Stams—Maricopa. Curtis notes: "This individual exhibits strongly the characteristics of the Yuman stock to which he belongs." To emphasize, Curtis removed Western clothing and photographed him against a dark background with harsh lighting. Published in *The North American Indian*, Supplement to Volume II. *Library of Congress, Prints & Photographs Division, Edward S. Curtis Collection, LC-USZ62-106800*

Right: Hoo-Man-Hai—Maricopa. Photographed in a head-and-shoulders portrait, this Maricopa Indian sports a full, bushy mustache and modern clothing—something Curtis frequently removed. c.1907. *Library of Congress, Prints & Photographs Division, Edward S. Curtis Collection, LC-USZ62-106254*

X2180-07

X2186-07

Above: Unsure of his surroundings, a small Maricopa child sits in a large, ornately woven basket. c.1907.
Library of Congress, Prints & Photographs Division, Edward S. Curtis Collection, LC-USZ62-123311

Right: Hipah with arrow brush—Maricopa. Of the Maricopa, this woman was one of Curtis' favorite subjects, with her long, wild hair and bright eyes. She appears in a number of photos. c.1907. Published in *The North American Indian*, Supplement to Volume II.
Library of Congress, Prints & Photographs Division, Edward S. Curtis Collection, LC-USZ62-115805

X2184-05

Above: A Yaqui Indian man, whom Curtis no doubt thought typified the Yaqui "type," sits for the camera wrapped in a blanket to emphasize his facial features. c.1907.
Library of Congress, Prints & Photographs Division, Edward S. Curtis Collection, LC-USZ62-104491

Right: Havachach—Maricopa. In a more formal setting, but wrapped in the same blanket, the woman pictured on page 45 stares at the camera with mischievous intensity.
Library of Congress, Prints & Photographs Division, Edward S. Curtis Collection, LC-USZ62-136596

X2181-07

Left: In this case Curtis chose to contrast the dark features of this woman with a light-colored blanket in a tightly cropped image, giving her a more exotic, but slightly rougher look than the girl above. *Library of Congress, Prints & Photographs Division, Edward S. Curtis Collection, LC-USZ62-117000*

Above: Qahatika Maiden. In addition to using a lighter background and dark blanket, Curtis softened the focus of his lens to give this Qahatika girl a gentler look, which contrasted with her tribe's hardscrabble life. *Library of Congress, Prints & Photographs Division, Edward S. Curtis Collection, LC-USZ62-112214*

Right: In this image Curtis chose to use varied garments with highlighting, against a neutral background. Although effective, the fringe work at left is almost distracting. *Library of Congress, Prints & Photographs Division, Edward S. Curtis Collection, LC-USZ62-104492*

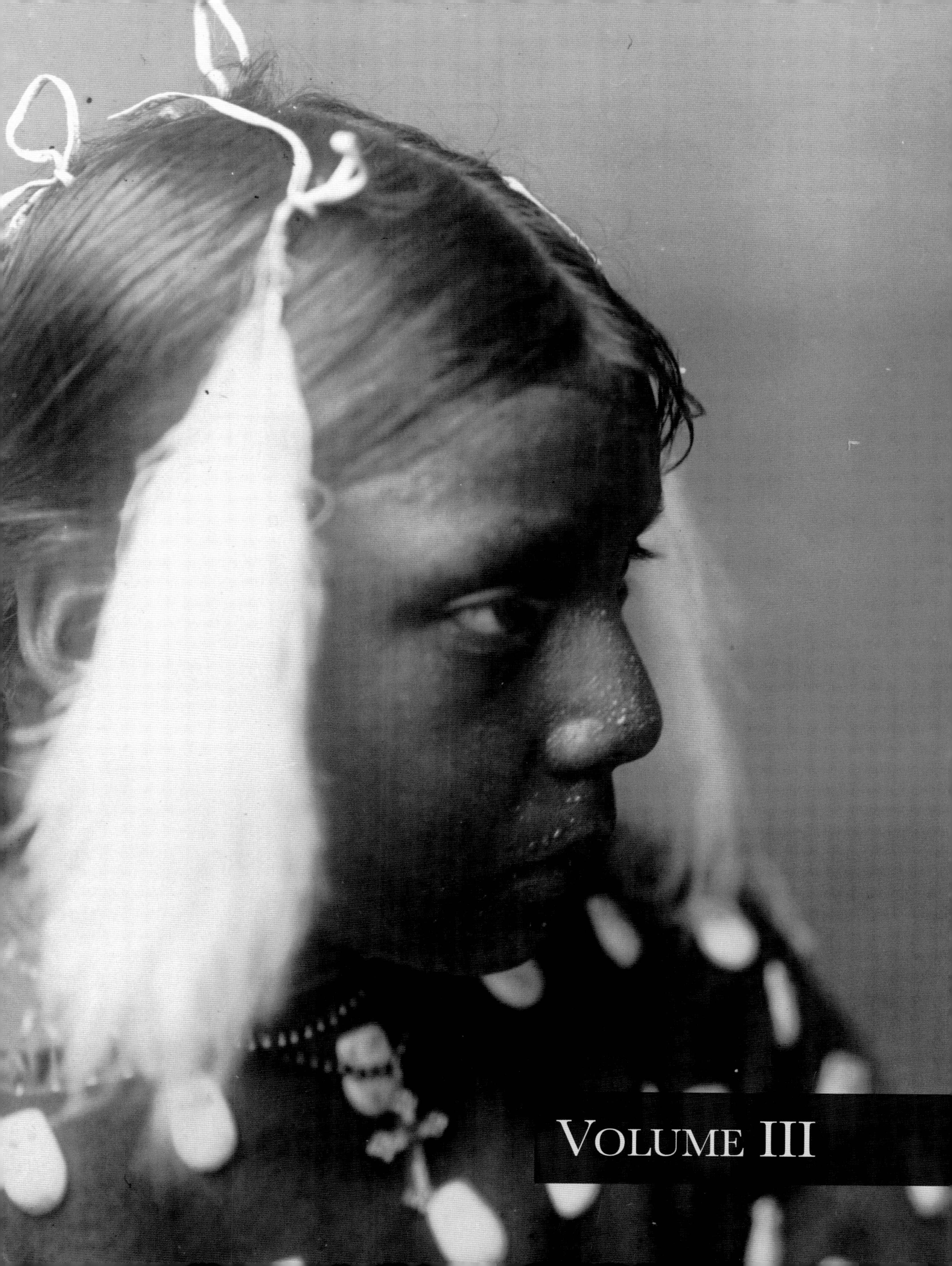
VOLUME III

VOLUME III

THE TETON SIOUX.
THE YANKTONAI. THE ASSINIBOIN.

PUBLISHED 1908

The third volume of *The North American Indian* focused primarily on Northern Plains tribes of the Dakotas and Montana. It was the second volume released in 1908 (most of the work was completed 1905–08), as Curtis was still hopeful of meeting his five-year deadline agreement with financier J.P. Morgan, not realizing the project wouldn't be completed for nearly another quarter of a century. By the time Curtis reached these tribes, most were living on reservations and had adopted many of the customs and dress of the White man. Many of the illustrations and extra gravure portfolio prints were portraits taken in his studio tent or were re-creations of battle scenes of years past. Despite the relatively fresh pain of the Wounded Knee massacre, the Indians re-created battles and cooperated fully with Curtis. He also recorded many songs of the tribes and completed biographies of a number of the aging warriors, including Red Hawk, Slow Bull and Iron Crow. Many of the men present had fought Custer at Little Bighorn and almost all were survivors of 1890's Wounded Knee Massacre. He also hired three Crow Scouts—Goes Ahead, Hairy Moccasin and White Man Runs Him to describe the Custer battle from their view as Custer's Scouts. Curtis was among the first to note that Custer needlessly sacrificed his men for a personal agenda. It also was during the 1907 field season that Curtis nearly lost his son, Harold, to typhoid, and marked the last time his wife, Clara, ever accompanied him into the field. Among the Sioux present who were most helpful to Curtis was Alexander Upshaw. Upshaw was a Carlisle graduate who also did post-graduate theological studies.

Previous Page: Named Woman of Many Deeds, Red Cloud's granddaughter appears in this unusual pose; a very close-cropped facial shot that is not quite a profile or three-quarters view. Her head is tilted down slightly with no eye contact, and she is wearing a cross.
Library of Congress, Prints & Photographs Division, Edward S. Curtis Collection, LC-USZ62-115800

Right: Curtis found the Sioux living in terrible poverty, but they were still a proud people. Red Dog (Shunka Luta) and others were pleased to be able to don traditional garb and relive the tribe's better days. In this close portrait he looks sad, but momentarily content.
Library of Congress, Prints & Photographs Division, Edward S. Curtis Collection, LC-USZ62-112246

Above: Yellow Horse, a Yanktonai, wears the tribe's traditional long braids, eagle feathers in his hair, and buffalo skin wrap. In this pose, taken in Curtis' field tent, Yellow Horse, an older man, has regained his proud countenance as he looks away from the camera. *Library of Congress, Prints & Photographs Division, Edward S. Curtis Collection, LC-USZ62-114840*

Right: This Sioux maiden, with long braids and dressed in beaded headband and beaded buckskin dress with shells, looks much like how Americans expected an Indian maiden to appear. c.1908. *Library of Congress, Prints & Photographs Division, Edward S. Curtis Collection, LC-USZ62-106267*

Below: Yellow Bone Woman and her family; 1908. She is wearing a horizontally strung "hairpipe" (tubular ornaments in bone) breastplate originally used for hair decoration (hence "hairpipes"). In this relatively informal family pose in front of a dwelling, the eye is drawn to her as the main figure.
Library of Congress, Prints & Photographs Division, Edward S. Curtis Collection, LC-USZ62-101183

Right: Black Eagle, an Assiniboin, is shown with his hair down, wearing a buffalo hide and holding the wing of a bird. Black Eagle's biography was given by Curtis. He was born in 1834, went to war at 13 and gained honors in later battles with the Yanktonai and Atsina, capturing horses and killing enemies. He married at 18.
Library of Congress, Prints & Photographs Division, Edward S. Curtis Collection, LC-USZ62-105371

Far Right: Ogalala Chief. By the time Curtis reached the Sioux in 1905, most of those who had survived Little Big Horn and Wounded Knee were old men. This aged Oglala chief, wearing a headdress and blanket supplied to him by Curtis, appears to be seeing something other than the camera.
Library of Congress, Prints & Photographs Division, Edward S. Curtis Collection, LC-USZ62-112240

Above Left: His Fights. His Fights was 76 in 1908, when Curtis photographed him. He took part in the Battle of Little Big Horn.
Library of Congress, Prints & Photographs Division, Edward S. Curtis Collection, LC-USZ62-83595

Above: Red Cloud. Chief Red Cloud is one of the most well-known of all Indian chiefs, mainly because of Red Cloud's War (1866–67), a series of conflicts that were later found to be caused by the Whites. In Curtis' portrait the chief appears thoughtful.
Library of Congress, Prints & Photographs Division, Edward S. Curtis Collection, LC-USZ62-66856

Left: Hollow Horn Bear, Brule. Although Hollow Horn Bear fought against the Whites in the 1870s, he eventually wanted to see peace. His characteristic features eventually graced a 14c postage stamp in 1923, and also appeared on a $5 bill.
Library of Congress, Prints & Photographs Division, Edward S. Curtis Collection, LC-USZ62-53674

Right: Elk Boy. For the portrait of Elk Boy, Curtis used a bright light and light garments to highlight the characteristic facial features of this warrior.
Library of Congress, Prints & Photographs Division, Edward S. Curtis Collection, LC-USZ62-121689

X2547-07

Left: Red Hawk. Red Hawk was an experienced warrior, who fought under Crazy Horse, then later, at Little Big Horn. With bright, diffused light he appears almost ethereal.
Library of Congress, Prints & Photographs Division, Edward S. Curtis Collection, LC-USZ62-110227

Above: Fast Elk. Fast Elk was among the many leaders and warriors Curtis profiled in volume III. This profile portrait calls attention to his deeply lined face.
Library of Congress, Prints & Photographs Division, Edward S. Curtis Collection, LC-USZ62-136579

Right: Calico, another old chief, is shown in this three-quarters view, wearing the same headdress as Red Hawk, who appears on page 60. Note what appears to be a law enforcement star on a pendant. Published in *The North American Indian*, Volume II.

Library of Congress, Prints & Photographs Division, Edward S. Curtis Collection, LC-USZ62-91033

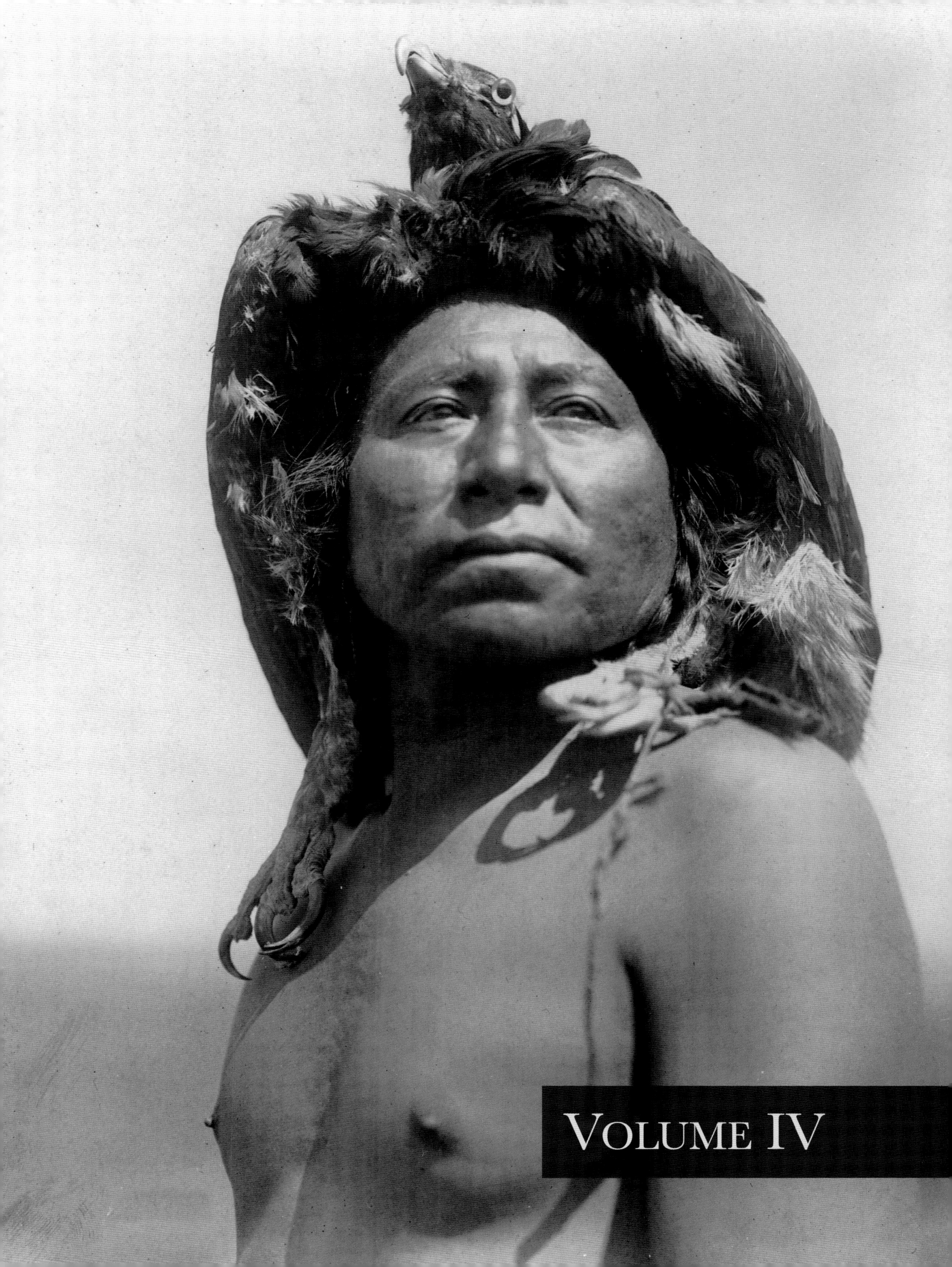

Volume IV

VOLUME IV

PUBLISHED 1909

Volume IV of *The North American Indian*, also set in the Northern Plains, was devoted to two tribes that were essentially one people. It was the first of two volumes released during 1909, the year Curtis and his wife officially separated. The Apsaroke (Crow) and Hidatsa tribes were two Siouan groups that had separated in recent enough history (sometime in the 17th century) that they were still well aware of their relationship to each other. These tribes had been decimated by smallpox about 70 years before Curtis arrived. Although the tribes were essentially friendly by the time Curtis arrived, the Apsaroke, a band of nomadic hunters in the mountains of Montana and Wyoming, looked down upon their "more sedentary" Hidatsa brethren, who were committed to agriculture, and who lived mostly along the Missouri River. Among the contrasts Curtis noted was a comparative vocabulary published as an appendix to Volume IV. While there are obvious language differences, much of the vocabulary is very similar in structure and pronunciation. Curtis again was aided greatly in the production of this volume by Alexander Upshaw, who appears in several of the photographs and gravures and served as both guide and interpreter. Upshaw, who fought against government agents to protect the reservation, was admired by his fellow tribesmen, but not local Whites. He was murdered in November 1909, and Curtis wrote of the importance of his friend in this volume. It was written mostly in October 1907 (along with much of Volume III), and Curtis and his crew worked 17-hour days, seven days a week. "Every thought and every moment had to be given to the work," Curtis noted.

Previous Page: This Crow medicine man wore a distinctive eagle headdress when he posed for Curtis in 1908. He is shown against a muted outdoors background, looking off in the distance.
Library of Congress, Prints & Photographs Division, Edward S. Curtis Collection, LC-USZC4-117711

Right: This head-and-shoulders portrait of Plenty Coups, a Crow, features him with a pompadour, traditional temple braids, beaded buckskin shirt and shell beads around his neck. c.1908.
Library of Congress, Prints & Photographs Division, Edward S. Curtis Collection, LC-USZC4-109715

X2808-08

Left: At the time Curtis photographed him, Lean Wolf was 88 years old and was the most authoritative living source of traditional Hidatsa culture. He is shown here wearing a horn headdress trimmed in white fur and dark feathers. c.1908.
Library of Congress, Prints & Photographs Division, Edward S. Curtis Collection, LC-USZ62-106293

Above: A portrait of a Mountain Crow man, Shot in the Hand, who was born around 1841. This profile portrait accentuates his facial features and pompadour.
Corbis

Far Left: Sitting Elk. In his eighties when Curtis photographed him, Sitting Elk told many stories. Among these was that he married at 34 and had 11 wives, 10 of whom he had "thrown away." c.1908.
Published in *The North American Indian*, Supplement to Volume IV.
Library of Congress, Prints & Photographs Division, Edward S. Curtis Collection, LC-USZ62-46979

Left: Old Dog. A portrait of an older Apsaroke man, wearing a fur hat, cloth neckerchief, and beaded buckskin shirt. Curtis gave a brief profile of him in Volume IV. c.1908.
Published in *The North American Indian*, Volume IV.
Library of Congress, Prints & Photographs Division, Edward S. Curtis Collection, LC-USZ62-99610

Left: White Man Runs Him. Curtis published a full biographical sketch of this Apsaroke Indian in Volume IV. He served under George Custer as a scout at Little Big Horn and even made a cameo appearance in a movie in 1927. c.1904.
Published in *The North American Indian*, Supplement to Volume IV.
Library of Congress, Prints & Photographs Division, Edward S. Curtis Collection, LC-USZ62-105384

Above: Choosing to show Wolf as an old warrior, Curtis posed him with traditional hair, body paint and strings of hishi necklace. He holds a spear at an angle that allows the eye to travel through the composition easily. c.1908.
Published in *The North American Indian*, Supplement to Volume IV.
Library of Congress, Prints & Photographs Division, Edward S. Curtis Collection, LC-USZ62-46962

X2685-08

Left: Bull Chief, an Apsaroke, is shown here, looking petulantly at the camera and wearing a buffalo bull horn headdress. He was said to have been born in 1825, making him about 83 when this portrait was taken. c.1908.
Published in *The North American Indian*, Supplement to Volume IV.
Library of Congress, Prints & Photographs Division, Edward S. Curtis Collection, LC-USZ62-46963

Above: Lone Tree (actually One Pine), was an Apsaroke medicine man attributed with having had the power to see the future. He once foretold the death of more than 100 Apsaroke and Atsina warriors, and is shown with an arrogant expression. c.1908.
Published in *The North American Indian*, Volume IV.
Library of Congress, Prints & Photographs Division, Edward S. Curtis Collection, LC-USZ62-109137

X1312-05

X2678-0B

Far Left: Alexander Upshaw, an Apsaroke had left his tribe to become educated and later returned, advoc for their well being. H served as guide and interpreter for Curtis two field seasons, but murdered by Whites in 1909. c.1905.
Published in *The North American Indian*, Supplement to Volume IV.
Library of Congress, Prints & Photographs Division, Edward S. Curtis Collection, LC-USZ62-124178

Left: Swallow Bird. This Crow Indian in Montana posed in a head-and-shoulders portrait for Curtis. He has a painted pompadour, Apsaroke headdress, Western-style button-down flannel shirt, beads on chest and a studded pipe held in front of his right arm. c.1908.
Library of Congress, Prints & Photographs Division, Edward S. Curtis Collection, LC-USZ62-106767

Above: Curley was a Crow Indian scout at the Battle of Little Big Horn. He is shown here in a full headdress, but wearing a Western-style button-down shirt. c.1905.
Library of Congress, Prints & Photographs Division, Edward S. Curtis Collection, LC-USZC4-8869

Right: Of this Crow Indian, Curtis wrote: "Medicine Crow participated in ten severe fights, killed three men, had two horses shot under him, and had the distinction of having 'thrown away' six wives." He has a "medicine bird" fastened to his head, which suits the profile composition well. c.1908.
Published in *The North American Indian*, Supplement to Volume IV.
Library of Congress, Prints & Photographs Division, Edward S. Curtis Collection, LC-USZ62-106886

Above: Bread, Apsaroke. Although Curtis shows this bold-looking Apsaroke in full headdress and regalia, his short biography states that Bread never fasted, nor did he achieve an honor.

Library of Congress, Prints & Photographs Division, Edward S. Curtis Collection, LC-USZ62-136597

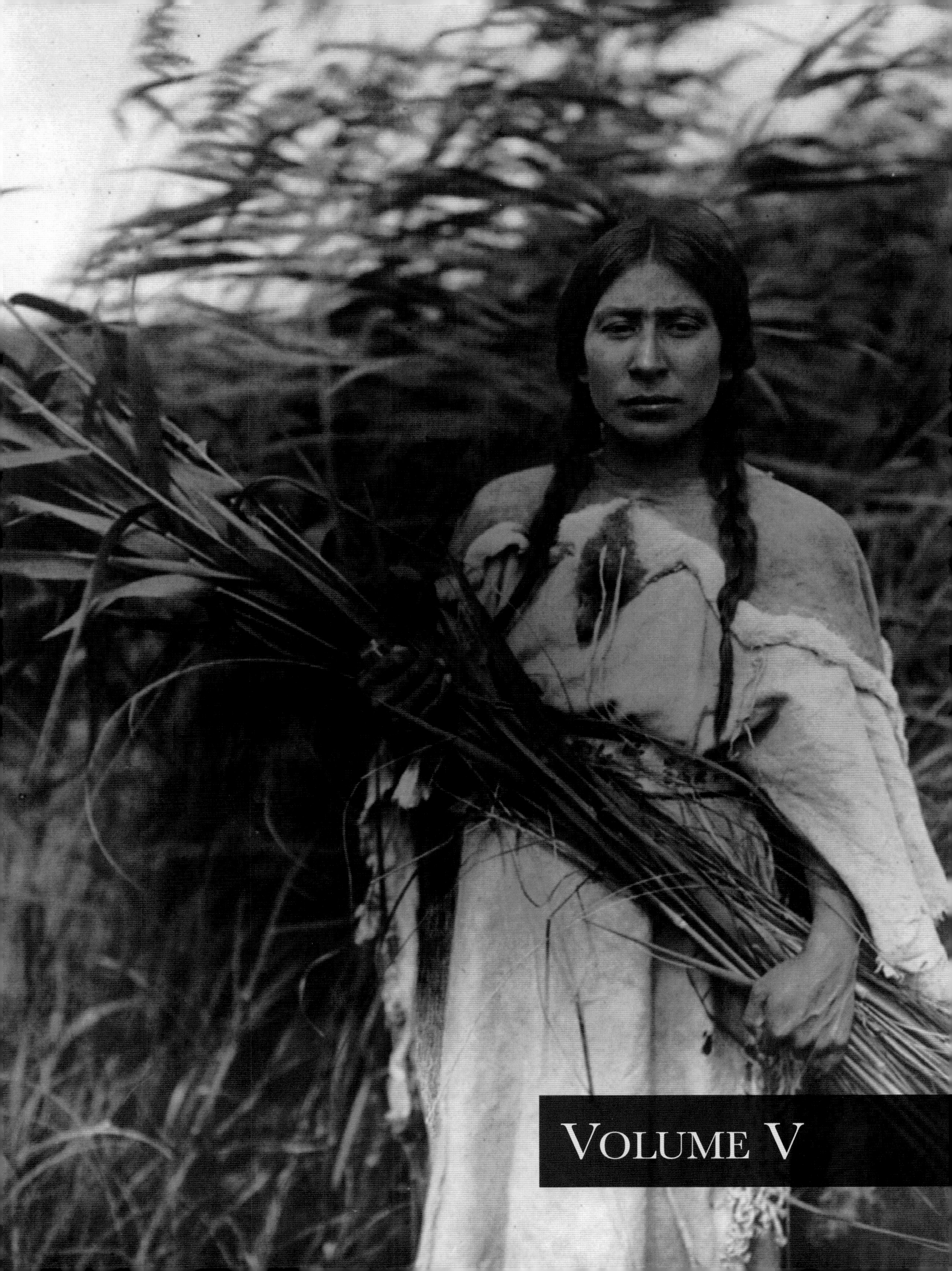

VOLUME V

VOLUME V

THE MANDAN.
THE ARIKARA. THE ATSINA.

PUBLISHED 1909

Volume V, covering tribes of the upper Missouri River Basin, was the second volume released in 1909, and the third with work completed in 1908. This was to fulfill Curtis' personal goal of finishing three books in a single calendar year. Unlike the Apsaroke and Hidatsa (covered in volume IV), who essentially shared the same language but differed greatly in lifestyle and habitat, the Mandan and Arikara in particular lived near each other and shared many similar cultural traits (most Whites couldn't tell the difference), but each had a separate language. The Mandan have always held a special fascination for many people, dating back first to the days of Lewis and Clark, who wintered among the tribe in 1804–05, then with George Catlin, who endeavored to show that they were of Welsh descent and went so far as to create a chart showing the ships that—in theory—brought the Mandan to North America. By the time Curtis visited, however, the Mandan had been so decimated by disease, war with the Sioux and contact with Whites that Curtis acknowledged there was "scant material for illustration." As a result, there is a great deal of text material in Volume V about the Mandan, but relatively few images. Many of the illustrations used for the book were of the Atsina (also known as the Gros Ventre). A total of 19 biographical sketches were included in Volume V, including Crow's Heart, Bear's Belly, Bull Neck, Red Star, Red Whip, Sitting Bear, White & Yellow Cow and Head Dress.

Previous Page: "The Rush Gatherer." An Arikara woman holds rushes, which were important to the tribe for weaving mats used as floor coverings. The tall rushes serve as an effective outdoor backdrop. c.1908.
Published in *The North American Indian*, Supplement to Volume V.
Library of Congress, Prints & Photographs Division, Edward S. Curtis Collection, LC-USZ62-77211

Right: Half-length portrait of Red Whip, an Atsina, seated, facing front, wearing a beaded buckskin shirt and holding a pipe in his left hand. Red Whip was born in 1858 and was well known for rushing his enemies, intimidating them and capturing their weapons. He served with General Miles and is said to have stopped the attacking Sioux while the troops escaped. c.1908.
Published in *The North American Indian*, Supplement to Volume V.
Library of Congress, Prints & Photographs Division, Edward S. Curtis Collection, LC-USZ62-105388

Far Left: Head Dress—Atsina. This nearly full-face portrait captures Curtis' portrait skills at their finest. Sharp, crisp facial details accentuate the Indian's intense gaze at the lens. c.1908. Published in *The North American Indian*, Supplement to Volume V. *Library of Congress, Prints & Photographs Division, Edward S. Curtis Collection, LC-USZ62-72451*

Left: Crow's Heart. This Mandan, with two eagle feathers, is wearing a buckskin shirt and necklaces, one made of bear claws. The perfect profile shows his characteristic high cheek bones and prominent nose. Published in *The North American Indian*, Volume V. *Library of Congress, Prints & Photographs Division, Edward S. Curtis Collection, LC-USZ62-52623*

Above: Sitting Bear —a portrait of an Arikara man. This full-front, straight-on portrait of Sitting Bear gazing into the camera is an enduring portrait style, with many details that accentuate his worn face.
Corbis

Right: This intriguing half-length portrait of Bear's Belly, an Arikara Indian, shows him wearing bearskin. It was shot against a neutral background that wouldn't compete with other design elements. c.1908.
Library of Congress, Prints & Photographs Division, Edward S. Curtis Collection, LC-USZ62-105497

Above: The focus of this half-length portrait of an Arikara woman is not as much on her facial features as on the six strands of hair pipe. She likely frequently wore her hair in that fashion. c.1908. *Library of Congress, Prints & Photographs Division, Edward S. Curtis Collection, LC-USZ62-101187*

Right: Looking tired, Eagle Child, an Atsina man shown in this profile wearing a buckskin shirt and headdress, was born in 1862. He was afforded a short biography near the end of Volume V. *Library of Congress, Prints & Photographs Division, Edward S. Curtis Collection, LC-USZ62-121686*

Above: White Shield, an Arikara man, c.1908. To many Whites, the Arikara were hardly distinguishable from the Mandan, among whom they lived, but Curtis found the Arikara to be a fascinating people with a different language and their own unique religious beliefs.
Library of Congress, Prints & Photographs Division, Edward S. Curtis Collection, LC-USZ62-125926

Right: Spotted Bull, one of the few Mandan Curtis was able to find to photograph for Volume V, appears in this profile, showing his neatly braided hair.
Published in *The North American Indian*, Volume V.
Library of Congress, Prints & Photographs Division, Edward S. Curtis Collection, LC-USZ62-83602

Above: Arikara Girl. This straight profile image is of an "Arikara type." To call attention to the girl's features, Curtis used a flat backdrop and a minimum of ornamentation.

Library of Congress, Prints & Photographs Division, Edward S. Curtis Collection, LC-USZ62-136594

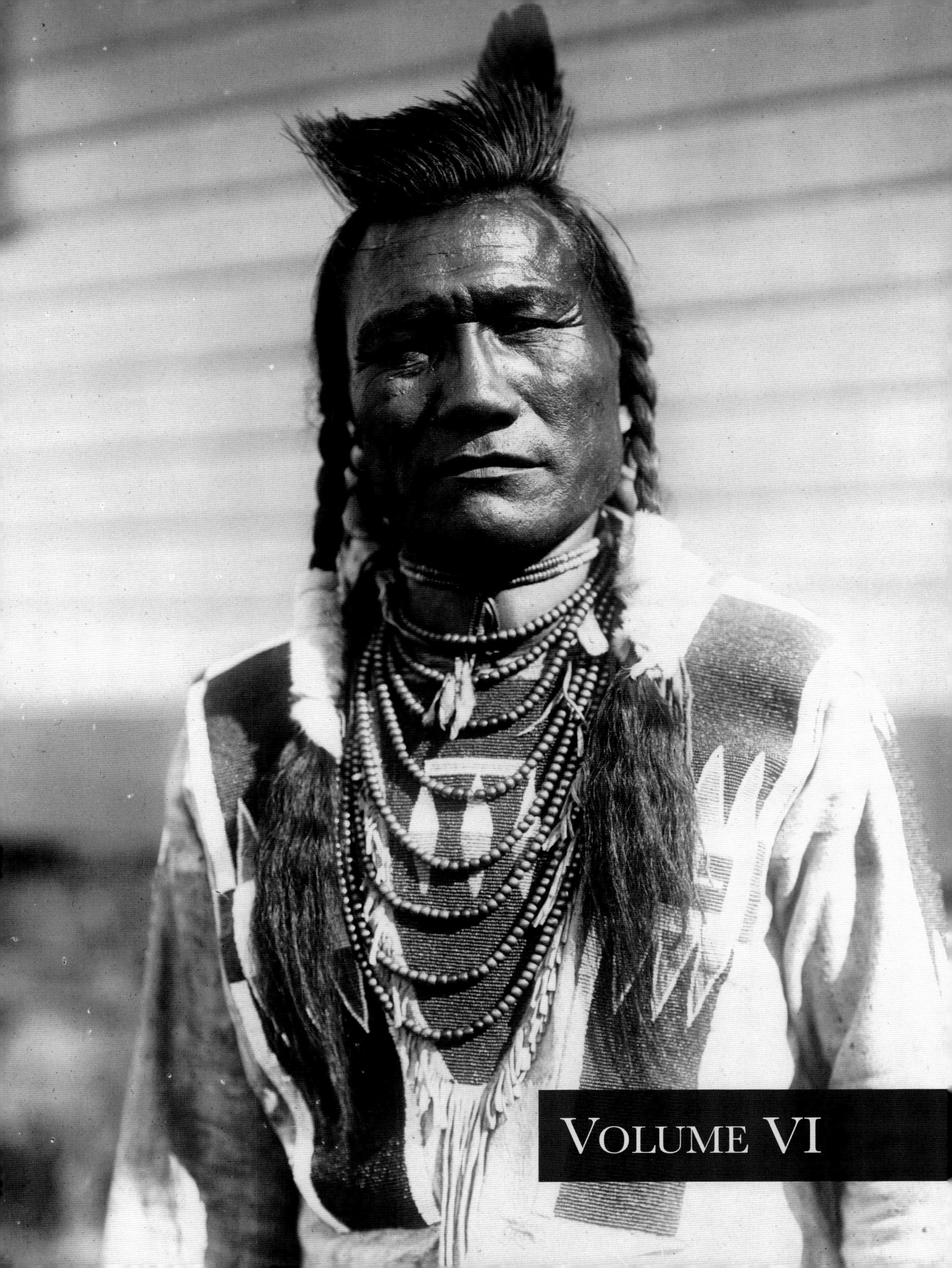
VOLUME VI

VOLUME VI

THE PIEGAN.
THE CHEYENNE. THE ARAPAHO.

PUBLISHED 1911

The period surrounding the completion of Volume VI and its release was an interesting time for Curtis. It was the fifth year of his planned five-year project. By the end of the year only eight of the planned 20 volumes had been released. Curtis continued to sink ever more deeply in debt, the project had already gone way beyond the costs he initially figured and his marriage was all but over. The Piegan were part of the Blackfoot family of tribes that Curtis first visited with George Bird Grinnell in 1900, which gave him the vision of his now-floundering project. Some of the photos and field work used in Volume VI were borrowed from that first and highly inspirational trip. Perhaps returning to the spot of inspiration helped to boost Curtis during this difficult time. Oddly, in this book, Curtis directed readers to consult the work of Grinnell, who had studied the Piegan for two decades. He stated that their stories and myths had "been so fully treated" by Grinnell that the space would be far better used by focusing on their religion, which Curtis did. But he still painted a very complete picture of the tribe, punctuated by a number of memorable images. The Cheyenne (northern band) and Arapaho are often grouped together as the same people because of their related languages, bison-oriented lifestyles and residence in Wyoming and southern Montana, but they were very different. In particular, the Cheyenne were very warlike and aggressively resisted White intrusion on their lands. When Curtis worked with them, the Cheyenne and Arapaho also shared the extreme poverty and greatly reduced numbers that had beset most of the plains tribes.

Previous Page: This half-length portrait of Bird Rattle, a Piegan man, shows him wearing a beaded buckskin shirt, feather, and a loop necklace. Although softened, the background appears to be a clapboard building, 1909.
Library of Congress, Prints & Photographs Division, Edward S. Curtis Collection, LC-USZ62-101251

Right: "The Ancient Arapaho." Curtis, like other photographers, was fascinated with deeply lined characteristic faces. In this portrait the subject has downcast eyes, is wearing plain clothing and is set against a neutral background to call full attention to the face, 1910.
Library of Congress, Prints & Photographs Division, Edward S. Curtis Collection, LC-USZ62-49040

Overleaf: Half-length group portrait of Reuben Black Boy and family, c.1910. The mixed styles of dress indicate what Curtis was facing at this point in the project—native cultures were quickly being overwhelmed by the White world. While visiting many tribes he struggled to find photographic subjects who still wore their clothes and hair in the traditional manner.
Library of Congress, Prints & Photographs Division, Edward S. Curtis Collection, LC-USZ62-112264

Left: Two Kill—a full-length portrait of the Piegan woman seated on blankets inside tipi, c.1910. The purpose of this portrait was to show a native habitat type. The full interior portrait (showing artifacts) downplays the individual, who does not have eye contact with the camera. *Library of Congress, Prints & Photographs Division, Edward S. Curtis Collection, LC-USZ62-117609*

Above: Mike Shortman. Described by Curtis as "Piegan man, half-length portrait, facing right," Mike Shortman is the epitome of what Curtis would have thought was a typical Piegan man. He has strong, almost Asian features, with a slightly flattened nose. c.1910.

Library of Congress, Prints & Photographs Division, Edward S. Curtis Collection, LC-USZ62-117608

Above: This Piegan woman is wearing a beaded deerskin dress with shells and delicate embroidery around the yoke. The camera angle (from slightly below the woman) is unusual. c.1910. Published in *The North American Indian*, Volume VI.

Library of Congress, Prints & Photographs Division, Edward S. Curtis Collection, LC-USZ62-115821

Right: A three-quarter-length portrait of Wild Gun and his family, likely taken inside Curtis' field tent. It is interesting to note that both Wild Gun and his wife appear to have sustained right-eye injuries at some point. c.1910.
Library of Congress, Prints & Photographs Division, Edward S. Curtis Collection, LC-USZ62-112266

Overleaf: Shown is Running Owl's family, an adult woman and two daughters, seated on a cloth on the floor of a lodge, wearing beaded cloth dresses. The beaded dress of the younger girl (center) appears to be the same as the one worn by Wild Gun's daughter on pages 100–101, and the lodge itself is the same as Two-Kill's (page 96–97). c.1910.
Published in *The North American Indian*, Volume VI.
Library of Congress, Prints & Photographs Division, Edward S. Curtis Collection, LC-USZ62-107614

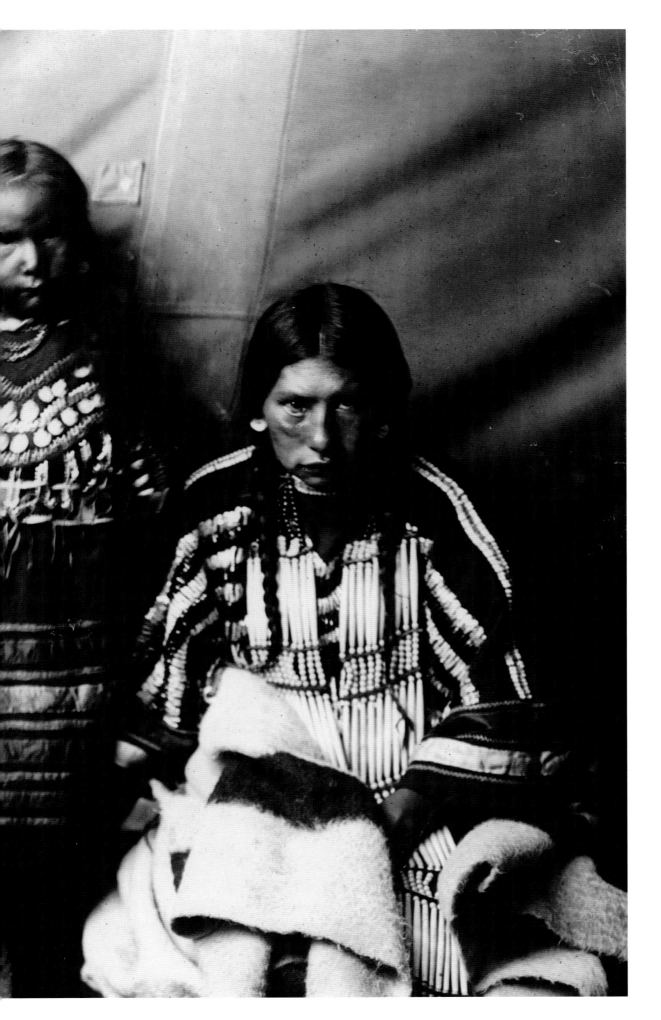

Far Left: A Cheyenne mother sits for Curtis, holding her child gently. Although you cannot see her eyes or her child, you can see the strong maternal love. c.1905. *Library of Congress, Prints & Photographs Division, Edward S. Curtis Collection, LC-USZ62-112271*

Left: Cheyenne Young Woman. Focusing again on a "type," Curtis accentuates the features of this young woman's face. She appears to be fairly heavily bundled. *Library of Congress, Prints & Photographs Division, Edward S. Curtis Collection, LC-USZ62-131461*

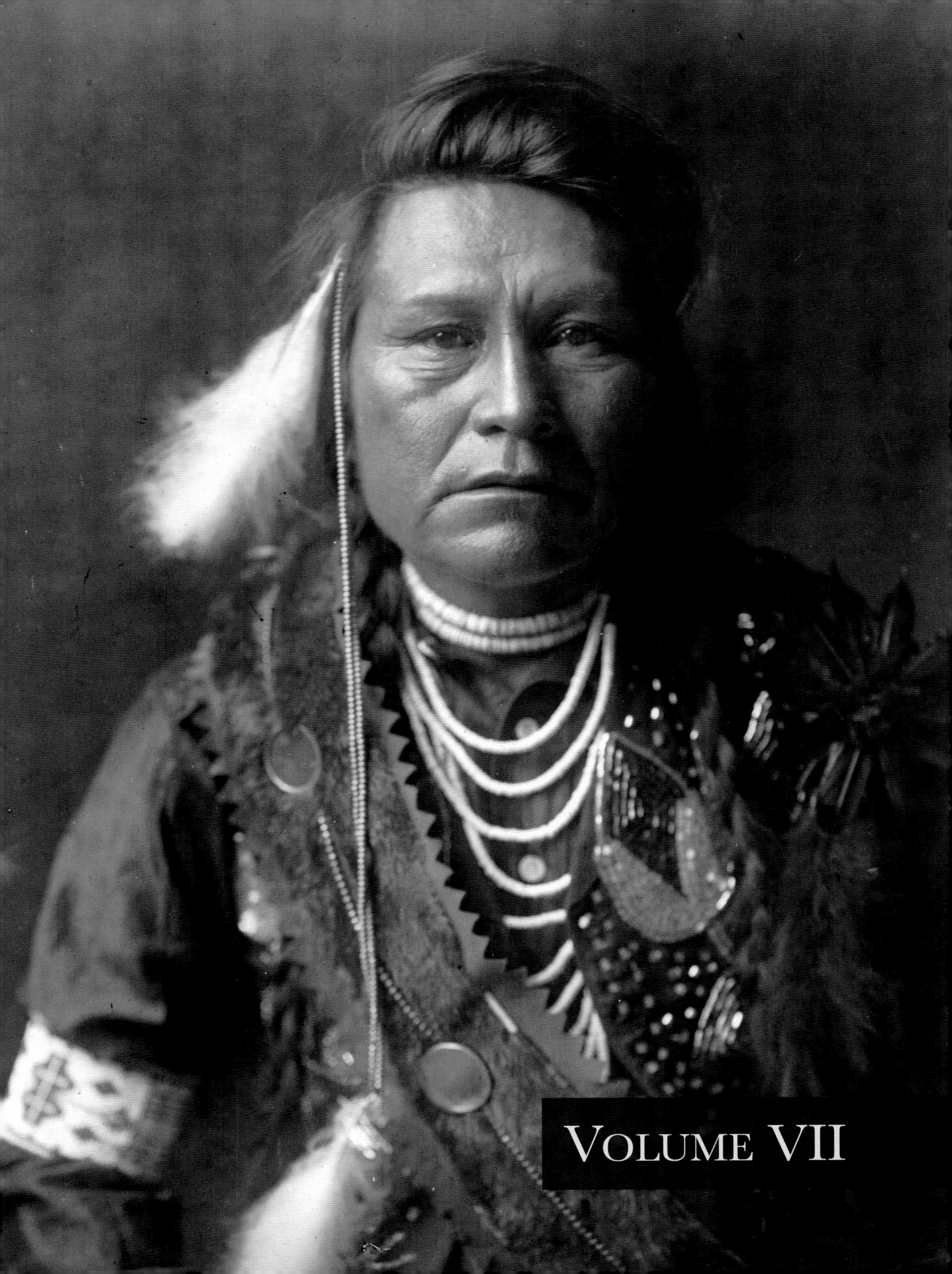
VOLUME VII

VOLUME VII

PUBLISHED 1911

Moving to the Columbia River Basin, encompassing an east-west area between the Eastern Rockies and Cascades (and between the 46th and 49th parallels, north-south), Curtis devoted Volume VII to a large group of small, related tribes, including the Yakima, Klickitat, Salishan (15 tribes) and Kutenai. Much of this work was completed in 1909. Of particular note is that all these people lived in areas that provided a far more naturally abundant lifestyle than many areas where Indians were living by the time Curtis arrived. The mighty Columbia River and its tributaries played an essential role in their lives, providing them with a rich supply of fish—their primary food source. Fertile woodlands and semi-arid plateaus were alive with still-abundant game, and there were plenty of sources for fruits, seeds, vegetables and nuts. Like many of the plains tribes, the Kutenai lived in tipis, but they were relatively sedentary, and Curtis wasn't impressed with them as a people for this reason. The range of the Salishan tribes spread from the Bitterroot Mountains of western Montana in the west to central Washington. Curtis focused on the easternmost tribes of the group, the Flatheads and Pend d'Oreilles (Kalispel), who had adopted aspects of plains culture, including bison hunting and tipi dwellings. The Yakima and the Klickitat lived farther down the Columbia Basin in south-central Washington, each residing near rivers. When Curtis and his assistant, William Myers, visited these people they had very separate lives, but later during the 20th century the Klickitat relocated to the Yakima reservation and culturally blended into the larger tribe.

Previous Page: Half-length portrait of Inashah, a Yakima man; c.1910. Although this man is dressed in his tribal finery, a button-down flannel shirt can be seen under the man's necklaces.
Library of Congress, Prints & Photographs Division, Edward S. Curtis Collection, LC-USZ62-119409

Right: Half-length portrait of the wife of Mnainak, c.1910. The collective name "Yakima" has for many years been used to designate all the confederate groups on the agency built around the true Yakima, which also includes some Wishram (or Wishham) and Wasco of Chinookan origin.
Library of Congress, Prints & Photographs Division, Edward S. Curtis Collection, LC-USZ62-115806

X3176-10

Left: A formally dressed Flathead woman is standing near a tree holding her baby in a cradleboard in front of her in this full-length portrait, 1910.
Library of Congress, Prints & Photographs Division, Edward S. Curtis Collection, LC-USZ62-115804

Above: Flathead childhood. This full-length portrait of a Salish boy, posed wearing a costume and headdress, is likely one of the happiest, most exuberant portraits taken by Curtis of the Indians, c.1910.
Library of Congress, Prints & Photographs Division, Edward S. Curtis Collection, LC-USZ62-98071

Left: Touch Her Dress. A shy, young Kalispel girl (likely a "Kalispel type") is shown sitting on her knees, hands folded in her lap, c.1910. *Library of Congress, Prints & Photographs Division, Edward S. Curtis Collection, LC-USZ62-113092*

Above: This Kalispel young woman, Skohlpa (Dusty Dress), is garbed in a dress ornamented with shells that imitate elk tusks. The braids of hair are wound with strips of otter fur, and a weasel skin dangles from each. The bands of white on the hair were created with white clay. *Library of Congress, Prints & Photographs Division, Edward S. Curtis Collection, LC-USZ62-111294*

Above: Klickitat type, 1910. Curtis studied the facial structure and features of a number of the tribes he photographed during his work on *The North American Indian*. Those faces he found particularly characteristic were labeled "(tribe name) Type."
Library of Congress, Prints & Photographs Division, Edward S. Curtis Collection, LC-USZ62-136591

Right: Klickitat Profile, 1910. In some cases, such as with this aged Klickitat man, he did frontal and profile portraits, the subject wrapped in a plain blanket, eliminating all distracting elements.
Library of Congress, Prints & Photographs Division, Edward S. Curtis Collection, LC-USZ62-136589

Left: Flathead profile, 1910. Using sunlight (likely morning light), Curtis was able to capture all the nuances of this Flathead's facial features and hair. It is unknown why he chose not to photograph a simple profile.
Library of Congress, Prints & Photographs Division, Edward S. Curtis Collection, LC-USZ62-136602

Above: Flathead type, 1910. Despite being intended to be an ethnographic study of a native face, a great deal of character and personality of this Flathead man was captured by Curtis.
Library of Congress, Prints & Photographs Division, Edward S. Curtis Collection, LC-USZ62-136603

Above: Nespilim woman, 1905. As he did with many of the intriguing faces he found in the Southwest, Curtis wrapped this Nespilim woman's face in a blanket—both to draw attention to the features and to remove traces of modern life.
Library of Congress, Prints & Photographs Division, Edward S. Curtis Collection, LC-USZC4-8861

Right: Nespilim man, 1904. Curtis probably took this portrait as an ethnographic study, but the subject has his hair styled and is wearing a more formal outfit than in most "studies."
Library of Congress, Prints & Photographs Division, Edward S. Curtis Collection, LC-USZC4-8825

Above: Luqaiot—Kittitas, 1910. There is little doubt that Curtis simply could not resist taking a detailed portrait of this old Kittitas man, who not only communicates a quiet assuredness, but carries himself with dignity.

Library of Congress, Prints & Photographs Division, Edward S. Curtis Collection, LC-USZ62-136590

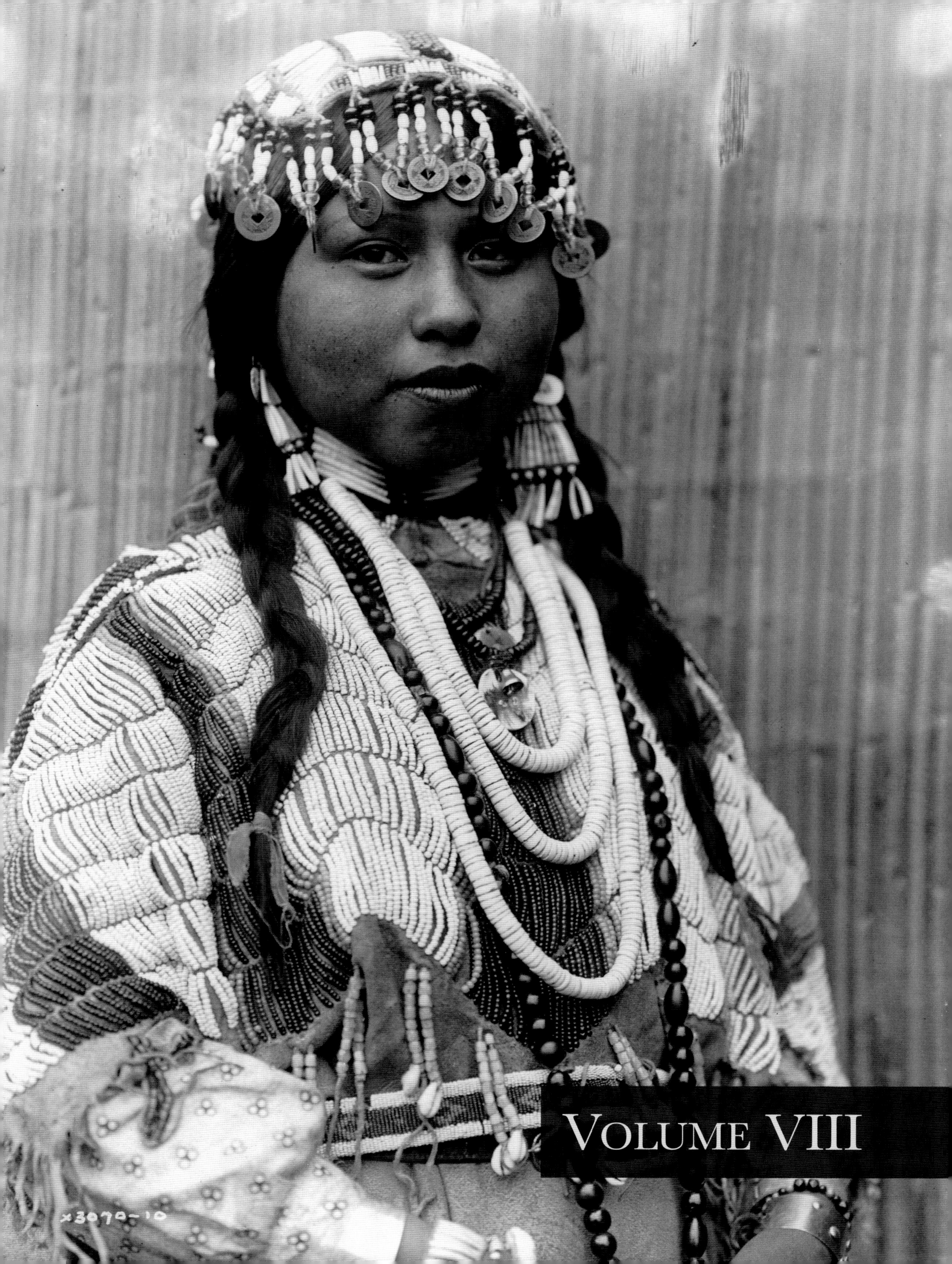

VOLUME VIII

VOLUME VIII

THE NEZ PERCES.
THE WALLAWALLA.
THE UMATILLA. THE CAYUSE.
THE CHINOOKAN TRIBES.

PUBLISHED 1911

Volume VIII was notable because it represented yet another cash infusion for the troubled and overdue project from investor J.P. Morgan. Work on the book was completed in 1909 and 1910. No profile of the Nez Perce would be complete without Chief Joseph, so Curtis used images of Chief Joseph he was fortunate enough to take in 1903, when he met and spent time with the aging chief (Chief Joseph died Sept. 21, 1904). Largely because of Chief Joseph, Curtis had a great deal of respect for the Nez Perce ("a much more vigorous people than their cogeners") and devoted much of the space in this volume to a tribe he likely would have included in Volume VII otherwise. In the book, Curtis explained that he wished to focus his reader's attention not on the details of their war of 1877 (and unsuccessful attempt to escape to Canada), but on the Nez Perce people, providing a forum for "the Indians' side of the story." He also noted the difference between the "Christian" and "heathen" factions of the tribe. Volume VIII also is significant for its coverage of the Wishram people, of whom Curtis became enamored. Curtis declared that readers "will be refreshed by a change to a life radically different from that of any tribe hitherto treated." He was clearly smitten with the salmon-fishing Chinook people who believed in magic and paddled large, distinctive canoes. Although he also covered the Wallawalla, Umatilla and Cayuse (the latter two whom he felt had nearly completely merged), they received less coverage.

Previous Page: A Wishram bride, c.1910. Curtis found that Wishram marriages were strictly business, with the families negotiating a suitable price for the bride, usually by messenger. This young Wishram bride is wearing a headdress with Chinese coins and a beaded dress—items all undoubtedly obtained by bartering their surplus salmon for goods delivered by visiting traders.
Library of Congress, Prints & Photographs Division, Edward S. Curtis Collection, LC-USZ62-105387

Right: Portrait of a young Wishram woman with braids, shell bead choker, and abalone shell disk earrings, c.1910. Stong backlighting calls attention to profile features.
Library of Congress, Prints & Photographs Division, Edward S. Curtis Collection, LC-USZ62-107917

Far Left: Nez Perce matron; c.1910. Other than this Nez Perce woman wearing more jewelry than she likely would normally have worn, Curtis likely changed little about her garments and accessories.
Library of Congress, Prints & Photographs Division, Edward S. Curtis Collection, LC-USZ62-113085

Left: Innocence, an Umatilla girl; c.1910. For the photograph of this cute little Umatilla girl Curtis probably had her don her buckskin dress over her normal Garment, a simple print dress.
Library of Congress, Prints & Photographs Division, Edward S. Curtis Collection, LC-USZ62-110503

Left: "A typical Nez Perce." Despite Curtis' title, there is little about this Nez Perce glaring at the camera in this full-face portrait that is "normal." He's wearing a full headdress, hairpipe choker and has his hair braided, c.1910.
Library of Congress, Prints & Photographs Division, Edward S. Curtis Collection, LC-USZ62-113086

Right: Three Eagles, an old man when photographed by Curtis, was a Nez Perce Indian who fought alongside Chief Joseph. In this portrait Curtis has given him a far-away look, c.1910.
Published in *The North American Indian*, Supplement to Volume VIII.
Library of Congress, Prints & Photographs Division, Edward S. Curtis Collection, LC-USZ62-111136

Far Left: Chief Joseph of the Nez Perce is one of the most well-known of all North American Indians. Curtis made friends with the old chief and had the opportunity to photograph him not long before Joseph's death in 1904, c.1903. Published in *The North American Indian*, Volume VIII.
Library of Congress, Prints & Photographs Division, Edward S. Curtis Collection, LC-USZ61-2088

Left: Youth in holiday costume—Umatilla. This young boy is wearing all the trappings, including a full headdress, strings of beads and an extensively beaded deerskin shirt. Curtis acknowleged it was a special costume, c.1910. Published in *The North American Indian*, Volume VIII.
Library of Congress, Prints & Photographs Division, Edward S. Curtis Collection, LC-USZ62-113088

Far Left: This Umatilla girl is shown in a full-length portrait, seated on the ground by a pine tree. She is wearing a fairly formal beaded blanket dress, beaded moccasins, and is holding a beaded bag in her lap. c.1910.
Published in *The North American Indian*, Volume VIII.
Library of Congress, Prints & Photographs Division, Edward S. Curtis Collection, LC-USZ62-111292

Left: his young Cayuse woman with braided hair is wearing hishi necklaces, a heavily beaded dress and elaborate sunburst earrings, c.1910. This is more formal dress than she would have worn on a normal day.
Library of Congress, Prints & Photographs Division, Edward S. Curtis Collection, LC-USZ62-109716

Above: Pounding fish. In this outdoors portrait of daily life Curtis photographed this woman grinding fish with mortar and pestle, dressed in a simple skirt and top, with a print bandana.
Library of Congress, Prints & Photographs Division, Edward S. Curtis Collection, LC-USZ62-113089

Above: The three-quarter-length portrait of this small Wishram girl shows her dressed in all her finery, including woven hat, dress, and beaded and woven belt. Note the silver coins on her hairpipe sash. *Library of Congress, Prints & Photographs Division, Edward S. Curtis Collection, LC-USZ62-105382*

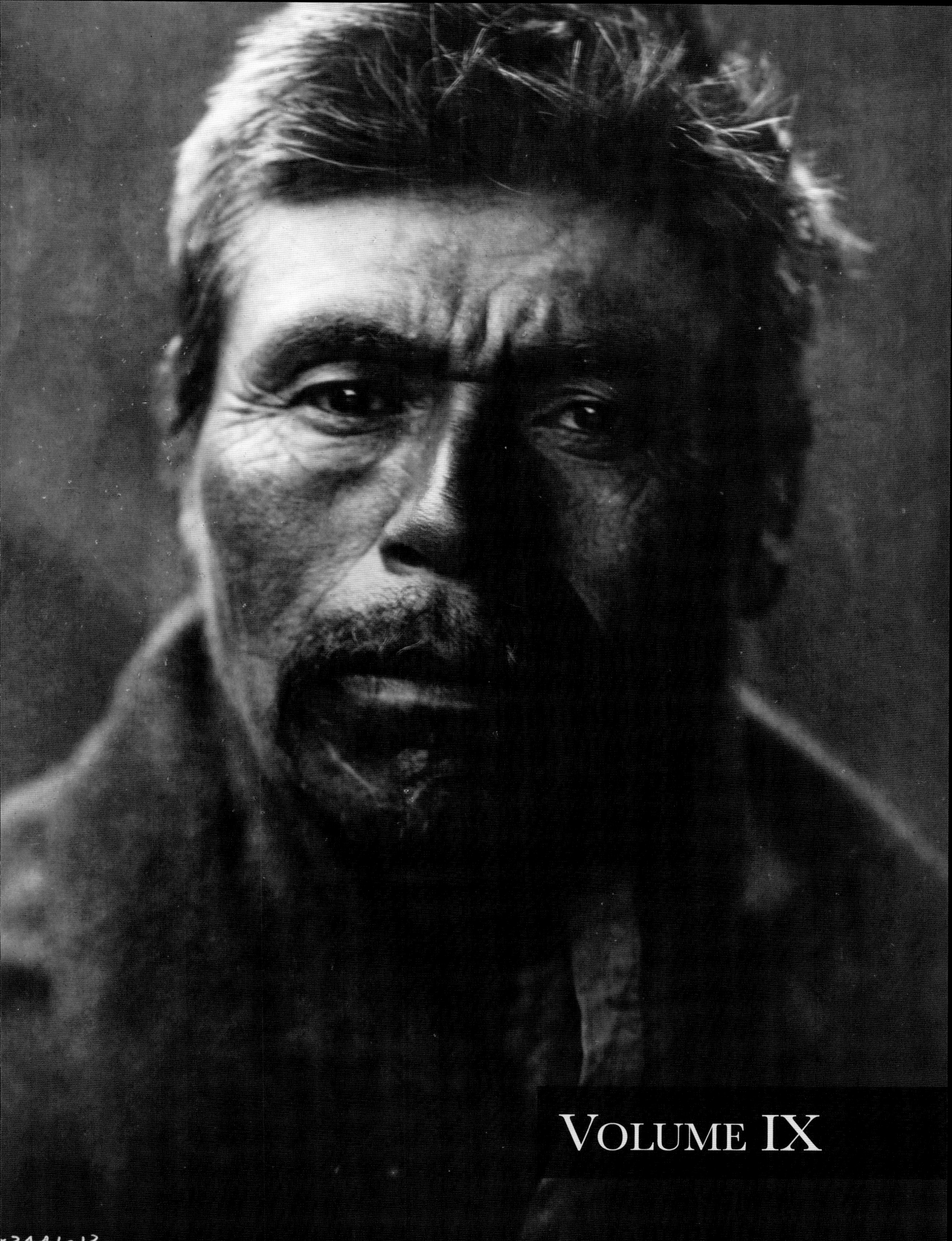

VOLUME IX

VOLUME IX

THE SALISHAN TRIBES OF THE
COAST. THE CHIMAKUM AND
THE QUILLIUTE. THE WILLAPA.

PUBLISHED 1913

This book was published two years after the release of Volume VIII (a year in which three volumes were released) and shortly after the death of Curtis' primary investor, J. Pierpont Morgan, on March 31, 1913. Curtis included a heartfelt tribute to his primary benefactor in the book. Volume IX, largely taken from fieldwork in 1910, also featured a few of his early photos. The work focused very specifically on the numerous small Salishan tribes living along the Pacific coast, almost exclusively in Washington, but extending northward past Puget Sound into British Columbia. Curtis was very familiar with some of these groups of Indians, having photographed them as early as 1896, as he was just beginning to truly become interested in Indians. These tribes were all united in speaking various dialects of the Salish language and by their similar cultures. All relied on the water for food; cedar for buildings, boats and implements; and on the potlatch ceremony for maintaining social order. Curtis was fascinated by these people, who he mentions were headhunters with "gruesome stories of primitive warfare." He also was interested by the fact these tribes were so completely dependent on sea food, "from clams to whales." The dense forest was extremely fertile, but with a ready supply of fish there was no incentive to develop an agricultural life, and they had little taste for land animals. This volume essentially set the stage for Volume X, which was drawn almost entirely from Curtis' work filming *Land of the Headhunters*, a 65-minute movie thought to be lost for many years and which was only recently restored, re-released and reunited with its original score by John J. Braham (1848–1919).

Previous Page: Silto, Quilliute. This man has a shorter, more modern haircut than many of Curtis' subjects, but he also has the deeply etched, weathered face common to many, c.1913.
Published in *The North American Indian*, Volume IX.
Library of Congress, Prints & Photographs Division, Edward S. Curtis Collection, LC-USZ62-132392

Right: "Shoalwater Bay Type." This close-up portrait of an older Indian focuses on his hair and facial features. A blanket has been pinned over his Western-style shirt. c.1913.
Published in *The North American Indian*, Volume IX.
Library of Congress, Prints & Photographs Division, Edward S. Curtis Collection, LC-USZ62-118575

Left: Basket maker—Skokomish. An old Skokomish woman is shown holding one of her baskets in this half-length portrait, c.1913. Although the focus is on the basket, Curtis effective captured the characteristic lines of the woman's face. Published in *The North American Indian*, Volume IX. *Library of Congress, Prints & Photographs Division, Edward S. Curtis Collection, LC-USZ62-118576*

Above: Quilliute girl; c.1913. This young Quilliute girl, covered by Curtis to feature her face, is wearing a slight smile. Curtis likely was struck by her dancing eyes.
Library of Congress, Prints & Photographs Division, Edward S. Curtis Collection, LC-USZ62-118580

Right: Young Quinault wearing shell ornaments; c.1913. This young Quinault girl was photographed by Curtis to show the finely beaded and strung hairpipe stole and her hairpipe headband.
Library of Congress, Prints & Photographs Division, Edward S. Curtis Collection, LC-USZ62-108467

Left: Quinault woman, c.1913. These peaceful people (Curtis uncovered evidence of only one minor battle in their recent history) lived quietly along the Washington coast between the Hoquiam and Queets rivers, catching salmon, trout, smelt, and other fish. This young woman is wearing the blanket and ornamentation over her Western clothes. *Library of Congress, Prints & Photographs Division, Edward S. Curtis Collection, LC-USZ62-108468*

Right: A Skokomish Indian chief's daughter, seated on canoe; c.1913. A large body of Salish on the Hood Canal, Washington, the Skokomish had wide trading ties, and a complex ceremonial and social structure including the use of slaves. In this "ethnological profile," the eye is drawn to the fur, canoe and basketry. *Library of Congress, Prints & Photographs Division, Edward S. Curtis Collection, LC-USZ62-110504*

Above: Curtis found the potlatch thriving with the Cowichan. The last day of these week-long ceremonies often included performances by masked dancers, such as this man photographed in June 1913. In this case the full-length portrait has nothing to do with the individual.
Library of Congress, Prints & Photographs Division, Edward S. Curtis Collection, LC-USZ62-52206

Above Right: Cowichan warrior's feather head-dress; c.1913. Again, while this is a full-face portrait, the young man is essentially a prop to model the headdress. He even wears a modern shirt.
Library of Congress, Prints & Photographs Division, Edward S. Curtis Collection, LC-USZ62-118582

Right: Quilcene boy. This young boy, with a full head of hair, sports two beautiful side braids, c.1913. He is wearing a blanket over his clothes.
Library of Congress, Prints & Photographs Division, Edward S. Curtis Collection, LC-USZ62-106996

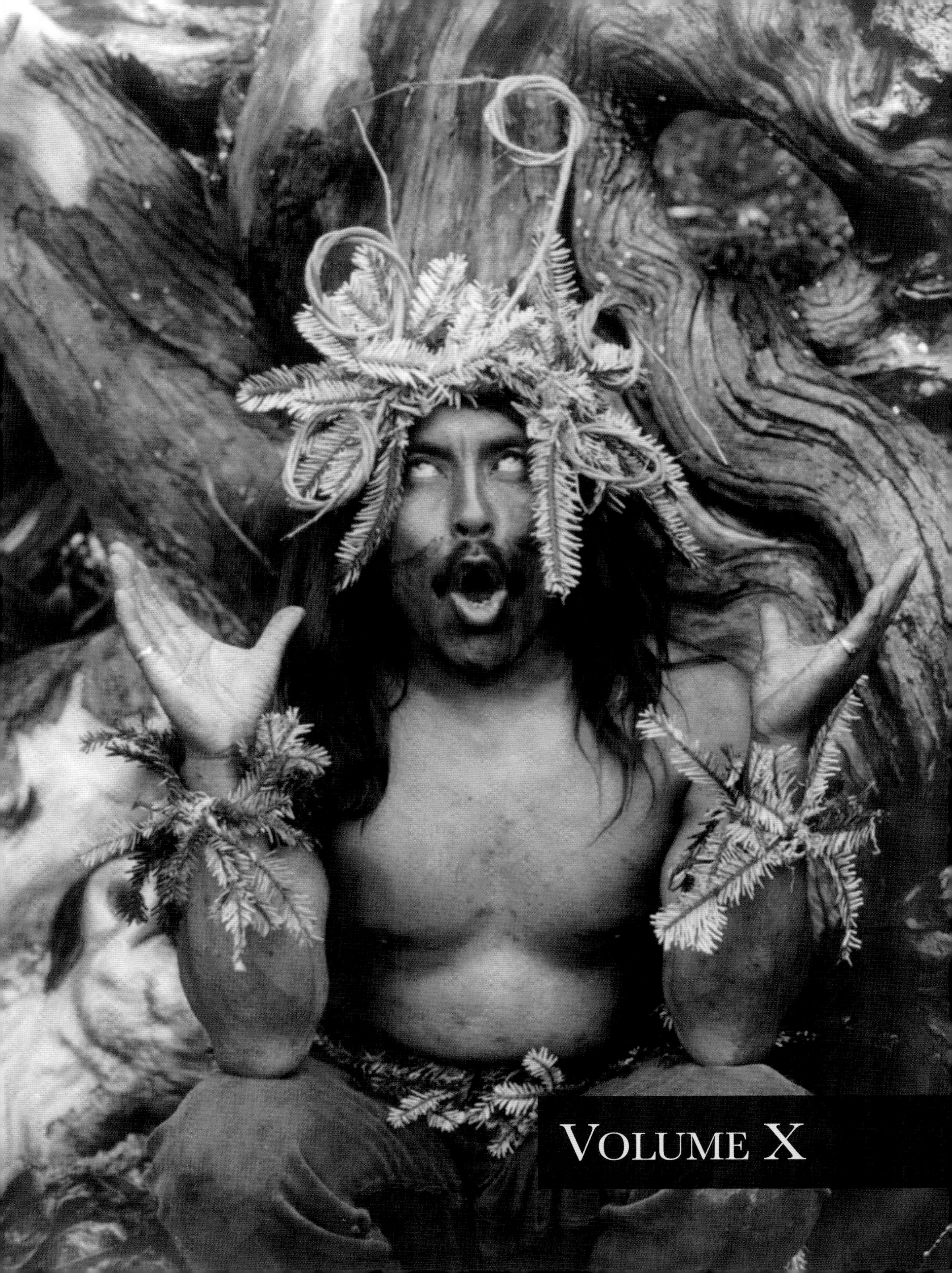

VOLUME X

VOLUME X

The cultural groups that form the various seafaring tribes of the North Pacific coast in British Columbia and on Vancouver Island were what Curtis had his lens aimed at during a portion of each fieldwork year between 1910–14. Very specifically, Curtis focused on the 34 tribes of the Kwakiutl. He justified this focus on the fact that theirs were "the only villages where primitive life can still be observed." His work on Volume X, which is half-again the size of its usually 200-page companions, is an almost stand-alone piece. It was even printed on thinner paper to accommodate the series' consistent volume size. The work also is the companion to Curtis' 1915 movie, *Land of the Headhunters*, which is finally acknowledged to be the first true ethnographic film. It was thought lost for many years, but in 1947, a single copy (rumored to have been found in a dumpster) turned up at the Field Museum in Chicago. The damaged and incomplete film was re-edited and released in 1974 as *In the Land of the War Canoes*. It was only recently reunited with its original score. Curtis formed the Continental Film Corp. and spent $75,000 filming the movie. In 1923, haunted by ever-mounting debt, he was forced to sell all rights for $1,500. The Kwakiutl had a rich mythology, complete with a legend of cannibalism within their secret society. Curtis supposedly partook in the "mummy eating" initiation into the Hamatsa secret society. "Whether I joined in the eating of the mummy or not I decline to answer," Curtis wrote. The Kwakiutl, for their part, were happy to participate in ceremonies and activities for which they otherwise would have been arrested. Curtis could not have succeeded with either the movie or the volume without the help of George Hunt, a half-Scottish member of the tribe, who also appears in some of the photos.

Previous Page: Hamatsa shaman, possessed by supernatural power after having spent several days in the woods as part of an initiation ritual; November 13, 1914. Curtis claimed to have become a Hamatsa during his time with the Kwakiutl, though he was secretive about his activities. He no doubt posed this individual in front of the gnarled tree to appear even more supernatural.
Library of Congress, Prints & Photographs Division, Edward S. Curtis Collection, LC-USZ62-52196

Right: Tsawatenok girl; c.1914. This full-front facial portrait of the young girl shows her wearing huge abalone shell earrings and a bark cape for wet weather.
Library of Congress, Prints & Photographs Division, Edward S. Curtis Collection, LC-USZ62-108465

Left: This individual, Curtis' half-Scottish Kwakiutl guide, George Hunt, is wearing a wig and modeling the costume of the Hamatsa secret society.
Library of Congress, Prints & Photographs Division, Edward S. Curtis Collection, LC-USZ62-113096

Above: Mask of the octopus hunter—Qagyuhl. In recording native ceremonial life Curtis occasionally took portraits of masks, such as this one, worn by a dancer during Tlu'wulahu, a four-day ceremony that preceded the Winter Dance to simulate the hunter who killed the man-eating octopus, c.1914.
Published in *The North American Indian*, Volume X.
Library of Congress, Prints & Photographs Division, Edward S. Curtis Collection, LC-USZ62-52213

Right: Tlahleelis—
Koprino. A number of
Curtis' close portraits
were taken to enable him
to practice physiognomy,
a then-popular means of
supposedly telling an
ethnic race's traits by
their physical features.
c.1914.
Published in *The North
American Indian,*
Volume X.
*Library of Congress, Prints
& Photographs Division,
Edward S. Curtis Collection,
LC-USZ62-52223*

Far Right: A Tluwulahu
mask—Tsawatenok.
Curtis' friend George
Hunt models a
Tluwulahu mask used
for a four-day dance
held before the winter
ceremony. The loon atop
the mask facilitates the
bird changing into a
man. Although the dance
is held by a secret society,
it is open to all, c.1914.
Published in *The North
American Indian,*
Volume X.
*Library of Congress, Prints
& Photographs Division,
Edward S. Curtis Collection,
LC-USZ62-47017*

Far Left: A chief's daughter—Nakoaktok. Although the full setting does not show in this image, the chief's daughter was photographed at a potlatch, where she was enthroned. She sits atop a platform supported on the heads of her "slaves", two carved images. c.1914. Published in *The North American Indian*, Supplement to Volume X. *Library of Congress, Prints & Photographs Division, Edward S. Curtis Collection, LC-USZ62-52204*

Left: Hamasaka, a Qagyuhl principal chief, in Tluwulahu costume with intricately carved speaker's staff and shaman's rattle, c.1914. This portrait says more about the costume than the subject. Published in *The North American Indian*, Supplement to Volume X. *Library of Congress, Prints & Photographs Division, Edward S. Curtis Collection, LC-USZ62-52212*

Above: The Hamatsa—Nakoaktok. A member of the Hamatsa
secret society, shown wearing a hat, c.1910. The hoop and blanket
appear to be the ones worn by George Hunt on page 146.
*Library of Congress, Prints & Photographs Division, Edward S. Curtis
Collection, LC-USZ62-101253*

X3340-10

VOLUME XI

THE NOOTKA. THE HAIDA.

PUBLISHED 1916

Volume XI appeared just a year after Volume X, focusing on other tribes that lived near the Kwakiutl; the Nootka and Haida. Much of the work on these groups was done concurrently with that accomplished for Curtis' film. Curtis took the photos, and William Myers did much of the ethnographic work and writing. Although Curtis was less than enthused with "the sleepy Indian village with a handful of mongrel inhabitants," he felt that Vancouver island's history was extremely important to the formation of North America as we now know it, and explained how the outcome could have been different. Beginning with 1774, when the Spanish, or as the natives called them, men in "steel shirts," landed on the island, there was a series of disagreements as to who owned the fur-rich land, including the Spanish, English and Russians. The Spanish ceded their interest to Britain in the 1785 Treaty of Nootka. Despite all the foreign contact, the Nootka retained much of their culture for more than a century. The Nootka, who lived mostly on the western shores of Vancouver Island, hunted sea otters, seals and whales; fished for cod and halibut; and were known for their exceptional basketry. The Haida lived farther to the north on the Queen Charlotte Islands. Their large and lavishly adorned community houses—and especially their stunning totem poles—made the Haida stand out. Volume XI was the last of the series to appear for a period of six years. Much of this can be attributed to World War I, which was fully raging at the time. Curtis' wife, Clara, also filed for divorce in what would become a very bitter and drawn-out struggle. Curtis would lose his house, studio, equipment and glass negatives in the settlement.

Previous Page: A Hesquiat maiden. The cedar bark ornaments on this young woman's hair were tied on the fifth morning of the Puberty Ceremony, to indicate a virgin, c.1910.
Published in *The North American Indian*, Supplement to Volume XI.
Library of Congress, Prints & Photographs Division, Edward S. Curtis Collection, LC-USZ62-118577

Right: This full-length portrait of a whaler from Clayoquot stands on shore with spear in hand. He is wearing a bark garment, c.1910.
Library of Congress, Prints & Photographs Division, Edward S. Curtis Collection, LC-USZ62-106742

Right: A young Makah girl sits for the camera, wrapped in a blanket. Curtis wrapped many subjects in a blanket to emphasize their facial features, c.1915. Published in The *North American Indian*, Supplement to Volume XI. *Corbis*

Above Left: "Oldest Man of Nootka." An elderly Nuu-chah-nulth man. Edward noted, "This individual is the most primitive relic in the modernized village of Nootka. Stark naked, he may be seen hobbling about the beach or squatting in the sun, living in thought in the golden age when the social and ceremonial customs of his people were what they had always been."
Corbis

Above Right: This full-front portrait of an old whaler in traditional hat and fur, looking off into the distance, gives almost an eerie appearance.
Corbis

Right: Portrait of a Clayoquot Girl. Published in *The North American Indian*, Volume XI.
Corbis

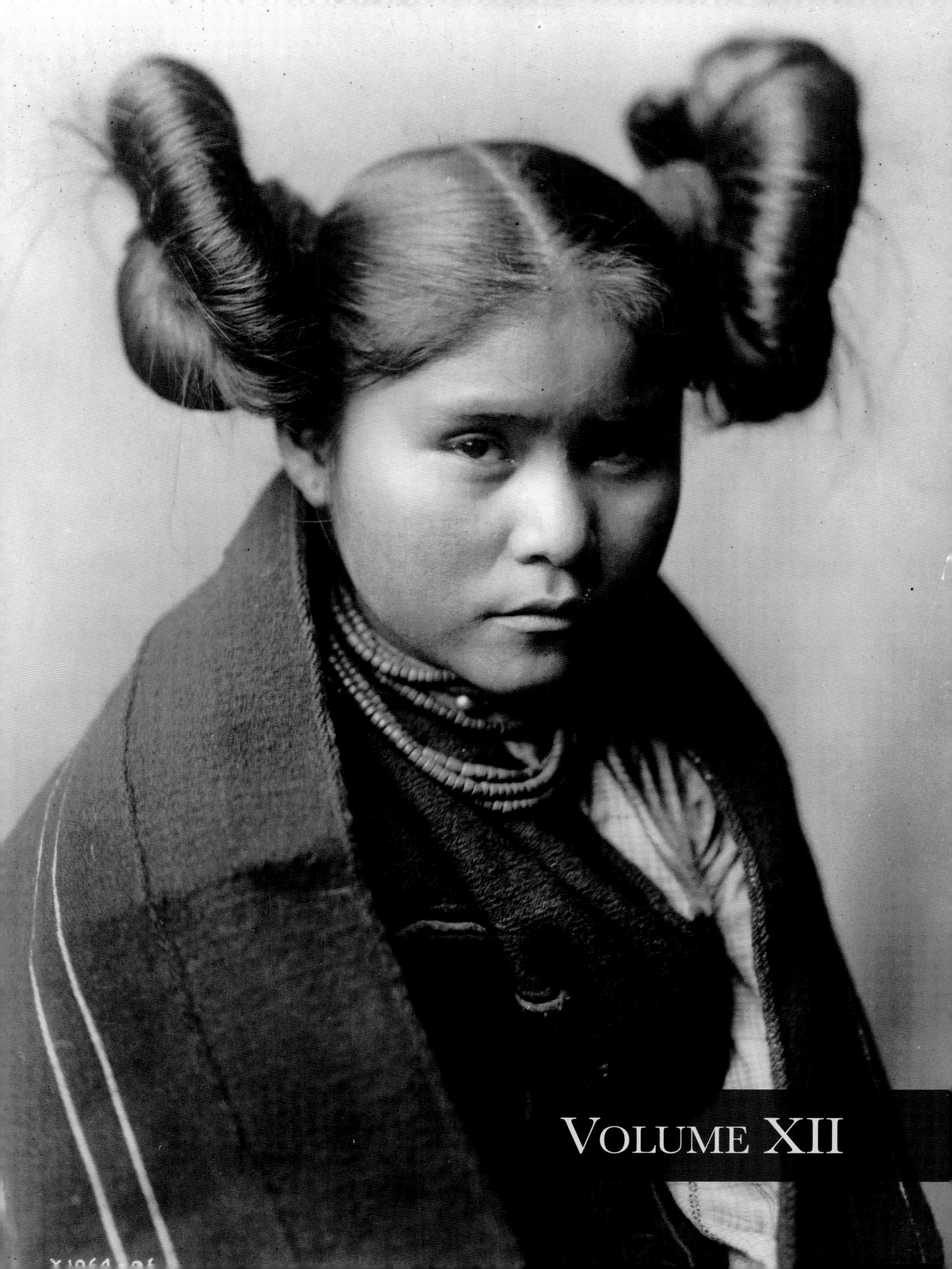

VOLUME XII

VOLUME XII

THE HOPI.

PUBLISHED 1922

From the Northwest Coast to the Southwest, Curtis returned once again to his favorite area for Volume XII to feature specifically the Hopi tribes of Arizona. He had visited the Hopi in 1900, 1902, 1904, 1906, 1911, 1912 and, finally, in 1919. The Hopi he found when he returned for this work were far different than those he'd left a few years earlier. The influence of Christian missionaries and the government had stripped the tribe of much its traditional culture. Curtis was hard-pressed to find Indians who had not adopted white clothing and hair styles. As a result, he relied heavily on photographs taken during his early visits, and he expressed gratitude for the images he'd captured more than a decade before. He also spent a fair amount of time shooting more or less candid shots of slices of native life, which he also had done in 1906, when he shot a series of portraits of two little girls, the "Moki Melon Eaters," among others. Walpi, the best-known of the Hopi pueblo villages, became Curtis' focus point, and he stated that unless noted otherwise, all references should be "considered as applying to this pueblo." In this volume he published a very complete description of the Snake Dance from his earlier experiences. Curtis had been adopted into the tribe during his 1906 visit and had actually participated in the Snake Dance at that time. He wrote that he would not have revealed this level of information while the priest who gave it to him was still alive.

Previous Page: Head-and-shoulders portrait of Chaiwa, Tewa girl, facing front, c.1906. The Hopis have lived in the same area of northeastern Arizona for more than 1,600 years. This young Hopi girl is shown in a traditional wedding outfit, with her hair in butterfly whorls.
Library of Congress, Prints & Photographs Division, Edward S. Curtis Collection, LC-USZ62-119411

Right: Nato, the Goat Man. In this half-length portrait of a Hopi man with animal skin, Curtis gives us a view of what a goatherd may have looked like before Whites arrived, c.1906
Library of Congress, Prints & Photographs Division, Edward S. Curtis Collection, LC-USZ62-112227

Above: "The Piki Maker." Piki is a form of blue corn bread that is wafer thin. The batter is spread by hand and the baked sheets are then folded and laid aside for future use. This young woman, known as Dayumana, had a daughter living as recently as 2000, c.1905. *Corbis*

Right: Tewa Girl. Although she doesn't look happy, this young Tewa girl is dressed in her wedding outfit, complete with butterfly hair whorls, ca.1906.
Library of Congress, Prints & Photographs Division, Edward S. Curtis Collection, LC-USZ62-105386

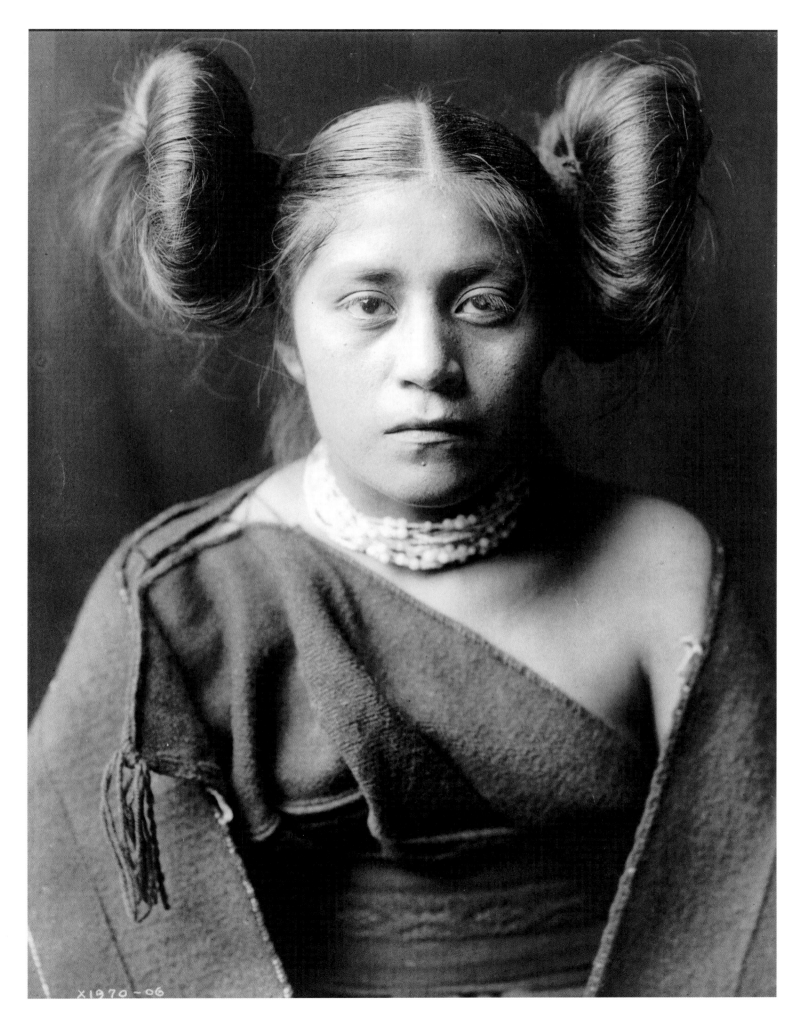

X1970-06

Right: This photograph shows a man from the village of Walpi, a Hopi pueblo founded in 1700 northeast of Flagstaff, Arizona. The young man is shown outside, with a muted background.
Christie's Images/Corbis

Far Right: In another portrait that is more about the activity than the model, Curtis captured this potter building her kiln. Southwestern potters fire their vessels in outdoor kilns. The type of material they burn with their pots helps determine the color of the finished objects, c.1906.
Published in *The North American Indian*, Volume XII.
Library of Congress, Prints & Photographs Division, Edward S. Curtis Collection, LC-USZ62-112110

COPYRIGHT
1909
BY E. S. CURTIS

Above: "Delights of Childhood." In one of his earlier visits, Curtis captured a series of several images of these two little girls messily eating a melon. The girl on the left stares suspiciously at the "Shadow Catcher," ca.1906.
Library of Congress, Prints & Photographs Division, Edward S. Curtis Collection, LC-USZ62-112224

Left: Honovi-Walpi snake priest. In this three-quarter-length view Curtis is recording the costume of the Snake Priest of Walpi, a small Hopi pueblo village in Arizona, ca.1910.
Library of Congress, Prints & Photographs Division, Edward S. Curtis Collection, LC-USZ62-117708

Above : The Snake Priest in action during a Snake Dance at the village of Walpi, c.1906.
Library of Congress, Prints & Photographs Division, Edward S. Curtis Collection, LC-USZ62-113080

Right: "A Hopi Man." This portrait, one of Curtis' more well-known images, was used in his writings on physiognomy, describing personality traits by facial features. The fact that Curtis was accurate in this case should be no surprise. This man was his friend, Sykyalestiwa, the Snake Priest who adopted him. *Corbis*

Below: Gobuguoy, Walpi girl. *Library of Congress, Prints & Photographs Division, Edward S. Curtis Collection, LC-USZ62-106758*

Left: Hopi Woman. A young Hopi woman, with her hair down, stares intently at Curtis' camera in this full-face half-length portrait, ca. 1904. *Library of Congress, Prints & Photographs Division, Edward S. Curtis Collection, LC-USZC4-8931*

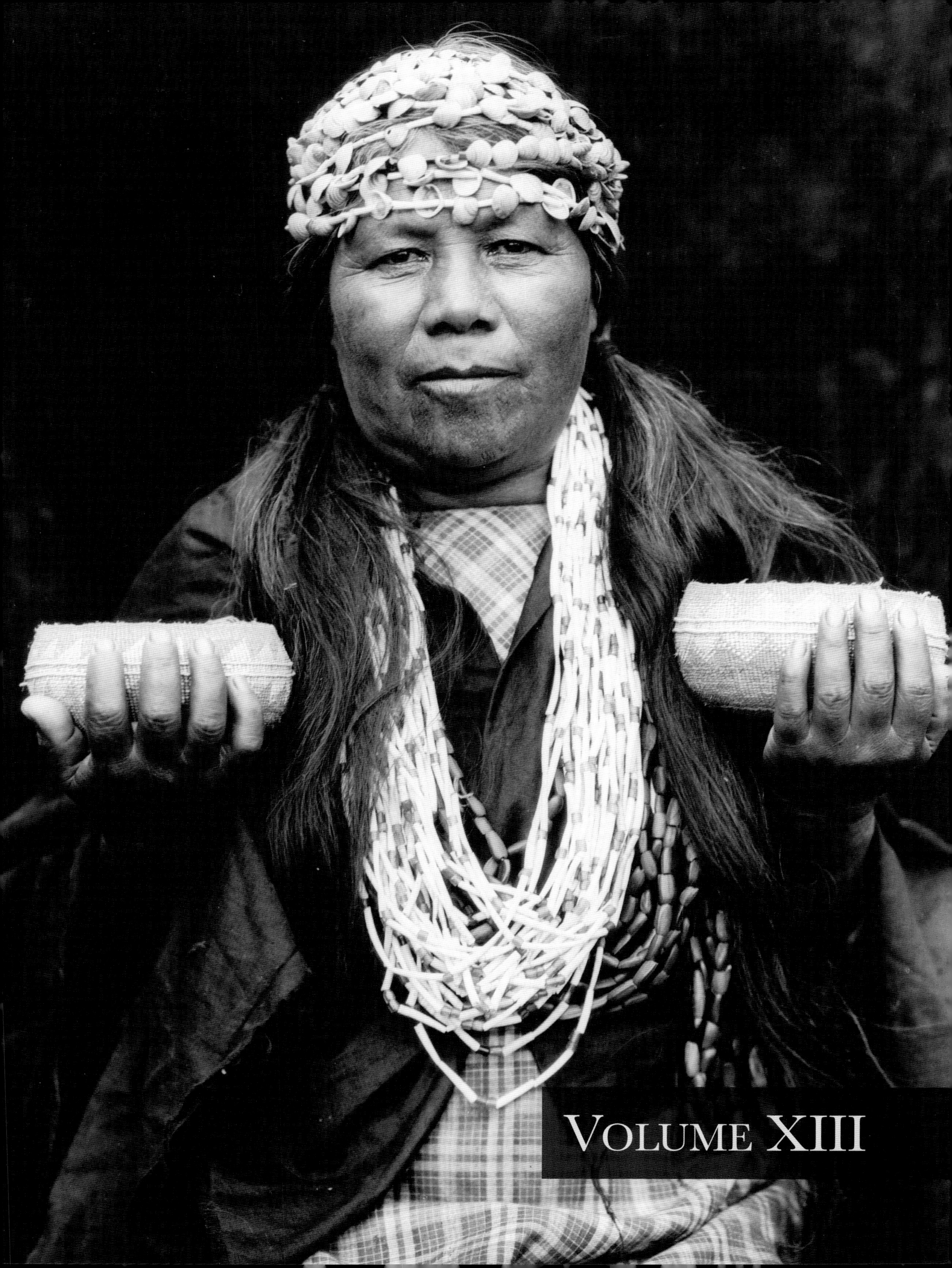
VOLUME XIII

VOLUME XIII

THE HUPA. THE YUROK. THE KAROK. THE WIYOT. THE TOLOWA AND TUTUTNI. THE SHASTA. THE ACHOMAWI. THE KLAMATH.

PUBLISHED 1924

By the time Volume XIII appeared, Curtis was continuing his slide into deep debt and was desperately trying to piece together the remainder of the project. He was already more than a decade overdue from the original five-year agreement, and still had seven volumes to go. The field work for this volume was conducted in 1916 and 1917 (by William Myers), but it was not until 1922 that Curtis was able to join him in the field to take the photographs. That year, Curtis and his daughter, Florence, traveled and finished the camera work for Volumes XIII and XIV. Curtis stated that the limits of this volume "are especially broad," including northern California, and Nevada to the Klamath Lake region of Oregon. By the time Curtis arrived, much of the Indians' historical material culture was already gone. Further, most of the tribes were living in some of most impoverished conditions, barely scraping survival from the land. Nonetheless, they still had a rich oral tradition. He spent a great deal of time photographing the tribes, pointing out the differentiating features of each, re-creating some scenes and shooting some modern life. What particularly sets volume XIII apart is the great deal of mythology he gathered from the tribes—about 40 pages in all. Included are stories explaining the cause of lightning, origin of tobacco and why frogs are in the water. In his introduction, Curtis not only decries the abject condition of many of these tribes, but asserts that California Indians likely suffered more under the White man than all other Indians, stating that "the author finds it difficult even to mention the subject with calmness."

Previous Page: Hupa shaman. Unusually, the Hupa recognized women in spiritual roles. Male Hupa shamans were rare. The Hupa lived along the lower Trinity River in what is now California and spoke Hupa, an Athabaskan language, c.1923. Published in *The North American Indian*, Volume XIII. *Library of Congress, Prints & Photographs Division, Edward S. Curtis Collection, LC-USZ62-101261*

Right: An elderly Hupa dancer is shown holding an effigy made from the head and skin of a deer. Effigies were used by many Indian tribes for protection or as a connection to the spirit world, c.1923. Published in *The North American Indian*, Supplement to Volume XIII. *Library of Congress, Prints & Photographs Division, Edward S. Curtis Collection, LC-USZ62-110226*

Far Left: Old Bob—Karok. Curtis was consistently fascinated with facial features. In this case he focused on Old Bob's deep-set eyes and lined face, c.1923. Published in *The North American Indian*, Volume XIII. *Library of Congress, Prints & Photographs Division, Edward S. Curtis Collection, LC-USZ62-118587*

Left: Woman's primitive dress—Tolowa. According to Curtis, this was "the gala costume of Coast Athpascan women. The ordinary dress was a deerskin kilt with the opening at the front protected by a fringed apron of deerskin or of bark," c.1923. Published in *The North American Indian*, Supplement to Volume XIII. *Library of Congress, Prints & Photographs Division, Edward S. Curtis Collection, LC-USZ62-113078*

Left: In this full-length portrait a Klamath man models a full costume, including leather gloves with a beaded leaf pattern, c.1923. Published in *The North American Indian*, Volume XIII. *Library of Congress, Prints & Photographs Division, Edward S. Curtis Collection, LC-USZ62-123299*

Above: A Klamath woman uses a pair of grinding stones to make meal, c.1923. In this outdoors profile portrait Curtis chose to partially obscure the face, leading the eye to the subject's hands. Published in *The North American Indian*, Volume XIII. *Library of Congress, Prints & Photographs Division, Edward S. Curtis Collection, LC-USZ62-115814*

Above: Achomawi mother and child, c.1923. These people were known popularly as Pit River Indians and they suffered somewhat less than most California tribes. The mother proudly holds her baby, who doesn't seem any too happy with the photographer.
Library of Congress, Prints & Photographs Division, Edward S. Curtis Collection, LC-USZ62-110225

Right: A Hupa woman wearing fur and beads around her neck and shoulders, c.1923. Probably the largest and most important Athabascan tribe in California, the Hupa or Hoopa lived principally on the Trinity River above its junction with the Klamath.
Library of Congress, Prints & Photographs Division, Edward S. Curtis Collection, LC-USZ62-105385

Far Left: Hupa in ceremonial White Deerskin Dance costume, c.1923. The Hupa, Yurok, and Karok had two major world renewal rituals, correlating with seasonal availability of major food resources: the Jumping Dance for the spring salmon run, and the Deerskin Dance for the fall acorn harvest and second salmon run. Performers held albino or other oddly colored deerskins aloft on poles, or carried obsidian blades covered with buckskin. Some, as here, wore wolfskin headbands and kilts of civet pelts. *Library of Congress, Prints & Photographs Division, Edward S. Curtis Collection, LC-USZ62-101260*

Left: Hupa mother holding baby, c.1923. The Hupa lived in small villages of rectangular plank houses, wore buckskin aprons and skirts, and excelled in basketry. These basketry skills are apparent in the baby carrier. *Library of Congress, Prints & Photographs Division, Edward S. Curtis Collection, LC-USZ62-110505*

Right: Hupa woman, c.1923. Curtis chose to photograph this older Hupa woman in a close-cropped three-quarters pose that features her face and part of her fur coat. *Library of Congress, Prints & Photographs Division, Edward S. Curtis Collection, LC-USZ62-115817*

Far Right: Klamath woman, c.1923. Over the years the Klamath became very mixed with Euro-Americans and lost much of their Indian culture, leading to the termination of the reservation's status and of all government programs and assistance by the Bureau of Indian Affairs. *Library of Congress, Prints & Photographs Division, Edward S. Curtis Collection, LC-USZ62-110506*

Right: Sam Lopez, head-and-shoulders portrait, wearing Tolowa costume including a redheaded woodpecker scalp headress and strings of dentalium shell beads, holding a traditional painted bow and an obsidian blade, a sign of wealth, c.1923. The Tolowa are an Athabascan tribe who occupied the Smith River drainage and some of the nearby coast in the extreme northeastern corner of California. Linguistically they were closer to the Rogue River tribes to the north than to their relatives to the south. *Library of Congress, Prints & Photographs Division, Edward S. Curtis Collection,*

Above: Old Klamath woman, c.1923.
Library of Congress, Prints & Photographs Division,
Edward S. Curtis Collection, LC-USZ62-136572

Above Right: Klamath man wearing headdress,
c.1923. In classic Curtis style, this portrait is so well
focused that one can count the stubble on the elderly
man's chin.
Library of Congress, Prints & Photographs Division,
Edward S. Curtis Collection, LC-USZ62-118598

Right: A Yurok widow; c.1923. Edward Curtis's
daughter, Florence, joined him on his travels among
the northern California tribes. She later recounted
her father's professionalism, describing him as a fast,
confident worker who displayed "none of the usual
fussing" she had seen from less-experienced
photographers. And what about his relationship with
his subjects? "He was friendly with the Indians, but
never personal. They seemed to sense his sincerity."
Library of Congress, Prints & Photographs Division,
Edward S. Curtis Collection, LC-USZ62-115818

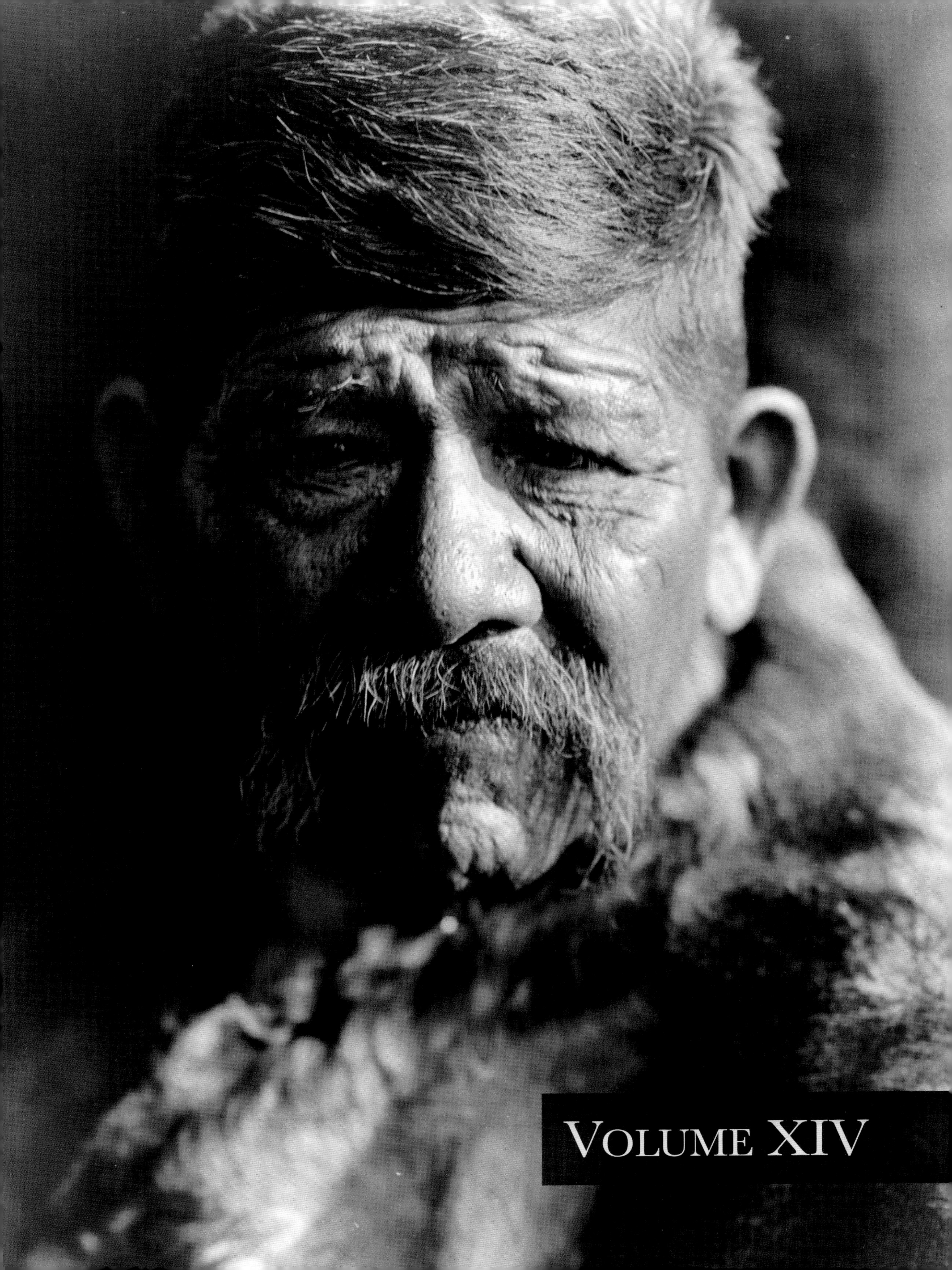
VOLUME XIV

VOLUME XIV

PUBLISHED 1924

Remaining in central California, but focusing to the south of areas covered in Volume XIII, Curtis focused on a number of fairly isolated hunter-gatherer tribes. Like their neighbors to the north, these tribes also were living in deep poverty, having been overrun early by the White miners and settlers. The remaining tribes lived in areas as varied as the redwood forests and the fertile Napa, Sonoma and Mendocino valleys, to the mountains of the Sierra Nevadas. In this volume, Curtis' tone toward the Whites becomes a bit more bitter. "The situation," Curtis wrote, "is a striking illustration of the recognized fact that the only Indians who received anything like fair treatment were the fighters, the tribes that killed ruthlessly and brutally. The peaceful Indians were driven from their lands, killed or outraged on the slightest provocation." It is the faces of some of the people in Volumes XIII and XIV that form a grouping of the most striking and heartbreaking of Curtis' portraits. Their faces show pain, anguish, hunger and exhaustion. Field work was done in 1915, 1916, 1922 and 1924. Curtis conjectured that "had the natives of California possessed the self-protective instinct of the plains tribes, the early history of the state, and in fact the United States, would read quite differently." But because these were small, isolated tribes with different linguistics and no overall larger social structure, they fell as "easy prey" to the White man. Like the northern tribes, much of their material culture was already gone, and Curtis gathered much of their mythology.

Previous Page: A Chukchansi chief, c.1924. The stress of his life and an unknown future is evident the eyes of this Chukchansi chief. His hair is cut in a more modern style.
Library of Congress, Prints & Photographs Division, Edward S. Curtis Collection, LC-USZ62-130202

Right: A Chukchansi (Yokut) woman, c.1924. By this time, Curtis' portraits had undergone a noticeable change. His romantic Indian images had been replaced by emotional photographs of suffering people. This change may have been an honest reflection of his subjects' poverty, but it may also have been a product his growing awareness.
Library of Congress, Prints & Photographs Division, Edward S. Curtis Collection, LC-USZ62-115813

Left: Miwok woman holding sifting basket, California, c.1924. This woman's gray hair and light garments, contrasting with her shadowy face, set off the appearance of the basket she's holding. *Library of Congress, Prints & Photographs Division, Edward S. Curtis Collection, LC-USZ62-114583*

Above: Man in Pomo dance costume with headbands of flicker feathers, c.1924. The social core of Pomo life was the family and the small village. Their beliefs were part of a religious complex called the Kuksu, which stressed curing rituals and elaborate forms of dancing and fire-eating to ensure the absence of danger from ghosts. *Library of Congress, Prints & Photographs Division, Edward S. Curtis Collection, LC-USZ62-110859*

Right: A Maidu man, c.1924. This Maidu man, wearing a modern shirt and hair style, also appears to be of mixed Mexican descent. He has very intense eyes. *Library of Congress, Prints & Photographs Division, Edward S. Curtis Collection, LC-USZ62-118595*

Above: Cecilia Joaquin, Pomo woman, using a seed beater to gather seeds into a burden basket, c.1924. In mild weather Pomos used little clothing; in cool weather they wore mantles, capes, robes and skirts of vegetable fiber or skins. Their fine baskets survive in quantity in museums.
Library of Congress, Prints & Photographs Division, Edward S. Curtis Collection, LC-USZ62-116525

Right: An old Yuki woman in mourning, c.1924. At the time Curtis photographed this old woman, she was one of only about 200 tribal members remaining. He was fascinated by her face.
Library of Congress, Prints & Photographs Division, Edward S. Curtis Collection, LC-USZ62-115809

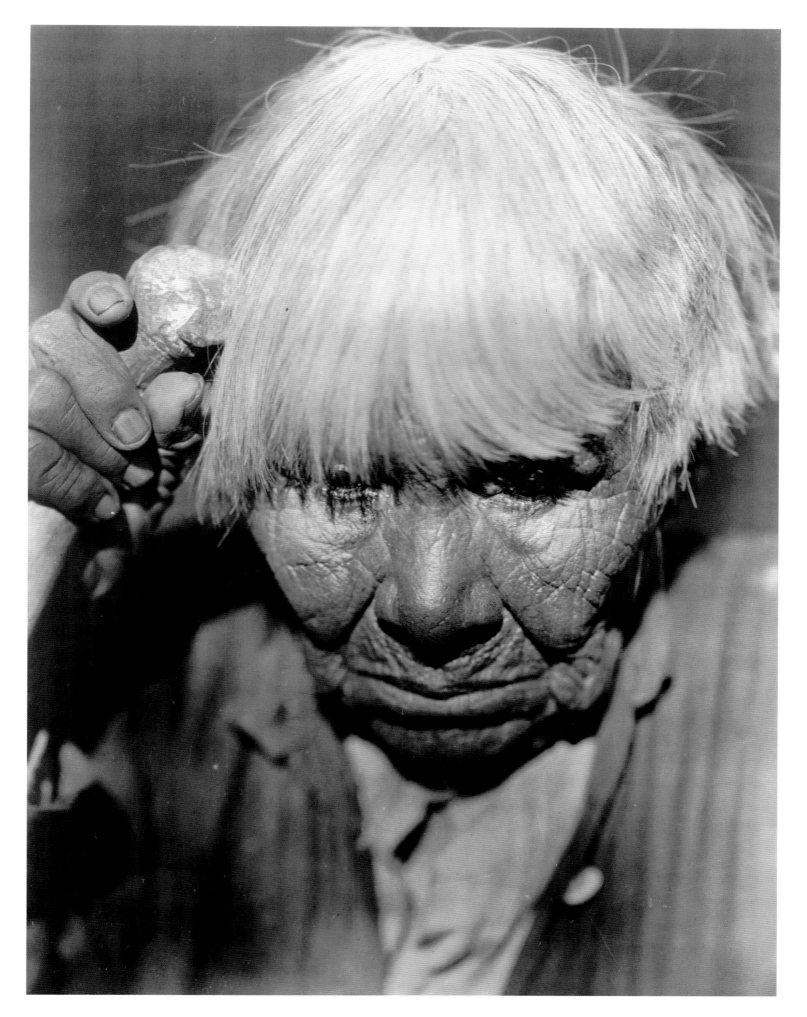

Left: A Kato woman, c.1924.
Library of Congress, Prints & Photographs Division,
Edward S. Curtis Collection, LC-USZ62-107616

Right: Standard garments for Wailaki men, according
to Curtis, included a small piece of deerskin, fur side
out, and a fur around the shoulders in cold weather,
c.1924.
Published in *The North American Indian*, Volume XIV.
Library of Congress, Prints & Photographs Division,
Edward S. Curtis Collection, LC-USZ62-118594

Volume XV

VOLUME XV

THE SOUTHERN CALIFORNIA SHOSHONEANS. THE DIEGUEÑOS. THE PLATEAU SHOSHONEANS. THE WASHO.

PUBLISHED 1926

In this, the first of three books published in 1926, Curtis examined the hunter-gatherer tribes of Southern California and Nevada. As sympathetic as he was to the Indians of northern and central California, Curtis was just as unsympathetic towards the natives he found in the desert land. "…one would suppose that, like Indians of similar environment elsewhere, they would have acquired at least the rudiments of agriculture," Curtis wrote. "On the contrary, they seem to have been contented to gain a livelihood by the least possible exertion," speaking of their diet of small mammals, reptiles, insects, larvae and the few seeds and fruits they could gather. As crude and as primitive as he found their culture, however, Curtis was extremely impressed by their basketry skills. He did admit, however (perhaps as an excuse for the delayed project), that "…the material has required a much longer time in the gathering than was found to be necessary in the case of some of the more populous tribes.…" The Diegueños and their Shoshonean neighbors, the Luiseños and Cahuilla, all lived in extreme southern California near the Mexican border. All were influenced by Spanish missions built in the region starting in the 18th century. By the time Curtis and Myers visited them, these tribes were an interesting mix of native and Spanish/Catholic culture. The Mono and Paviotso lived in small bands along the California-Nevada border. Speaking of these tribes, they "were inclined to be peaceable," according to Curtis, because "they had little to tempt the avarice of other Indians."

Previous Page: A Cahuilla woman, c.1924. This Takic-speaking tribe lived in the rugged desert north of Salton Sea in southern California. In describing how they dressed, Curtis noted "the subject of clothing could be ignored with little injustice to the Cahuilla"—traditionally they wore little or nothing.
Library of Congress, Prints & Photographs Division, Edward S. Curtis Collection, LC-USZ62-107207

Right: A Cupeño woman, c.1924. A small Takic-speaking tribe, the Cupeño lived east of Lake Henshaw and west of the Santa Rosa Mountains, California, and were closely related to the Cahuilla. They were missionized and reduced to the social status of near serfs during the Mexican and American periods.
Library of Congress, Prints & Photographs Division, Edward S. Curtis Collection, LC-USZ62-118585

Above: A Santa Ysabel woman; c.1924. The Diegueño or Ipai are a people occupying the border country of southern California in present San Diego County south of the San Luis Rey River—an area of coast, mountain and desert. They became part of the so-called "Mission Indians" of southern California, of both Yuman and Takic origin, who were to a large extent under the influence and control of the Spanish missions from 1769 until secularization during the Mexican period.

Library of Congress, Prints & Photographs Division, Edward S. Curtis Collection, LC-USZ62-115820

Above: Serrano woman of Tejon, c.1924. The Serrano were gatherers, hunters, and fishers; family dwellings were usually circular willow structures covered with tule thatching. The close full-front portraits of the two old women on these pages represent the deeply lined and care-worn faces that Curtis encountered regularly in the elderly.

Library of Congress, Prints & Photographs Division, Edward S. Curtis Collection, LC-USZ62-115825

Left: A Lake Mono basket-maker, c.1924. Although this is a large, profile portrait, the focus is on the woman's work, rather than her profile. Some of the basket-makers Curtis encountered in this area were exceptional. *Library of Congress, Prints & Photographs Division, Edward S. Curtis Collection, LC-USZ62-118771*

Above Left: Chemehuevi mother and child, c.1907. The Chemehuevi of San Bernardino County, California, are related to the loose collection of Southern Paiute bands of southern Utah and Nevada, including parts of Arizona above the Colorado River.
Library of Congress, Prints & Photographs Division, Edward S. Curtis Collection, LC-USZ62-112235

Above Right: Curtis said of this Washo basket-maker, "The coiled baskets produced by this woman have not been equalled by any Indian now living. About ninety years old, Datsolali appears to be in the early sixties. She has the pride of a master in his craft, and a goodly endowment of artistic temperament."
Library of Congress, Prints & Photographs Division, Edward S. Curtis Collection, LC-USZ62-114784

Right: A head-and-shoulders portrait of a Serrano man from the Tejon Creek area of southern California, c.1924
Library of Congress, Prints & Photographs Division, Edward S. Curtis Collection, LC-USZ62-118581

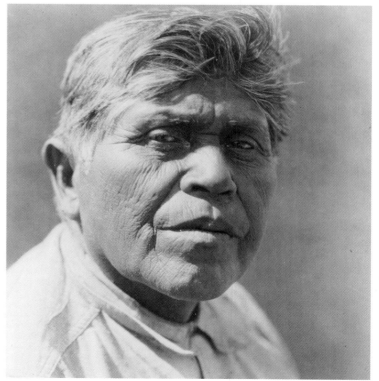

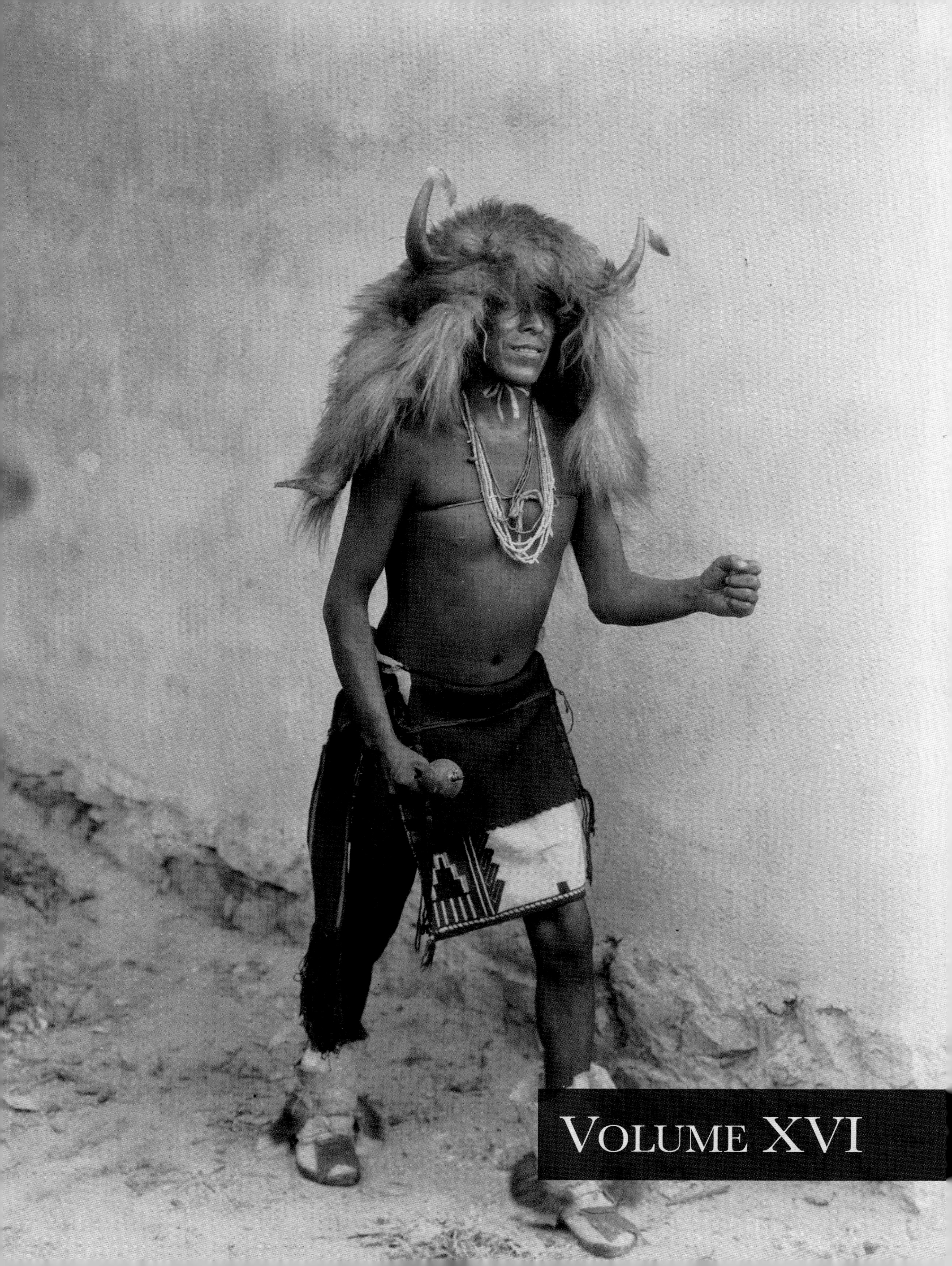
VOLUME XVI

VOLUME XVI

THE TIWA. THE KERES.

PUBLISHED 1926

Perhaps in his rush to finish the seemingly endless series, Curtis once again returned to the familiar Southwest (New Mexico) for Volumes XVI and XVII, but he also found the pueblo cultures extremely rich. "The full story of the Pueblo tribes of New Mexico will never be told, much less condensed into the two volumes of this work which are devoted to them." Curtis wrote. Indeed, New Mexico pueblo Indian culture was about as close to untouched as was possible at the time, despite contact with the Spaniards. Field work for this volume, which covers the linguistic stock of the Tiwa (Taos and Isleta pueblos) and Keres (Cochiti, Santo Domingo, Acoma and Laguna pueblos), was done in 1905, 1909, 1917 and completed in 1924. Most of the photos were taken either in 1904–05 or 1924. Of the pueblos covered in this volume Taos is likely the most well-known, and Acoma (the Sky City) has captured the imagination of thousands of people. Although most of the pueblo people have been peaceful for centuries, they were very protective of their religious rites and were known to kill violators. Using the fertile bottomland of the Rio Grande River, the agricultural pueblo Indians have always raised a wide variety of squash, corn and beans (the three sisters), as well as peppers and numerous other vegetables in more recent times. Most of the pueblos discussed by Curtis (which were several centuries old at the time) are still inhabited, although much of the reservation life has spread out from the central stacked adobe apartments. During 1924, when much of the work for these volumes was done, Curtis helped found the Indian Welfare League, which, among other things, was able to gain the vote for American Indians that same year as part of the Indian Citizen Act of 1924.

Previous Page: Sia Buffalo Dancer, c.1926. A Keresan-speaking Pueblo on the Jemez River about 30 miles north of Albuquerque, New Mexico, the Zia (or Sia) have gained a livelihood in the recent past from grazing sheep and goats on surrounding lands. *Library of Congress, Prints & Photographs Division, Edward S. Curtis Collection, LC-USZ62-106264*

Right: Head-and-shoulders portrait of an Acoma man, c.1904. This young man is wearing a bandana, a blanket over his clothes and is staring thoughtfully at the camera. *Library of Congress, Prints & Photographs Division, Edward S. Curtis Collection, LC-USZC4-8928*

Right: Shuati, a Sia woman standing, with pot on head, c.1926. The Zia are noted for making fine pottery with white or yellow-buff backgrounds with varied naturalistic designs of deer, birds and leaves. She also is wearing squash-blossom necklaces, the beads of which were often pounded from coins.
Library of Congress, Prints & Photographs Division, Edward S. Curtis Collection, LC-USZ62-106263

Far Right: Jemez Indian; c.1926. The people of this pueblo speak Towa, a dialect of Tanoan. The pueblo is located on the Jemez River 30 miles northwest of Bernalillo, New Mexico. Like many of the northern Pueblos, they were participants in the Pueblo Revolt of 1680 and suffered the traumas and punitive expeditions that followed.
Library of Congress, Prints & Photographs Division, Edward S. Curtis Collection, LC-USZ62-108424

Right: An Isleta woman poses, standing in a doorway and smiling broadly at the camera. This is one of the more candid-looking portraits taken by Curtis, c.1926. *Library of Congress, Prints & Photographs Division, Edward S. Curtis Collection, LC-USZ62-107615*

Far Right: A Taos girl, c.1905. Traditionally one of the more prosperous communities, surrounded by fertile agricultural land, this impressive multi-story pueblo is about 600 years old. It is geographically close to the Plains Indians, from whom the tribe adopted elements of material culture. Curtis noted that Taos men, in particular, could have been easily mistaken for Cheyenne in the way they dressed and carried themselves. *Library of Congress, Prints & Photographs Division, Edward S. Curtis Collection, LC-USZ62-106253*

X 1634-05

Above: Walvia ("Medicine Root"), a Taos woman. Curtis commented that it was very challenging to interview Taos people and learn their customs. The young seemed especially afraid of talking to Curtis and earning the wrath of their elders for sharing tribal secrets. This young woman looks less afraid in the photo on the facing page.
Library of Congress, Prints & Photographs Division, Edward S. Curtis Collection, LC-USZ62-106985

Right: Walvia ("Medicine Root"), c.1905. Curtis was clearly intrigued by young "Medicine Root." She is shown in both close-up and half-length portraits, modeling different garments.
Library of Congress, Prints & Photographs Division, Edward S. Curtis Collection, LC-USZ62-106990

X1633-05

Above: Iahla "Willow". Taken in Curtis' field tent, this portrait of "Willow," a young Taos Pueblo man features a draped head with a white cloth, which sets off the man's near-perfect facial features, c.1905.

Published in *The North American Indian*, Volume XVI.
Library of Congress, Prints & Photographs Division, Edward S. Curtis Collection, LC-USZ62-106255

1799-05

VOLUME XVII

VOLUME XVII

THE TEWA. THE ZUÑI.

PUBLISHED 1926

This installment, like Volume XVI, was devoted to New Mexico Pueblos, this time focusing on the linguistic groups of Tewa (San Juan, San Ildefonso, and Nambe pueblos), and the Zuni—a language, tribe and a pueblo all in one (in western New Mexico). Although he doesn't mention them specifically in his table of contents, Curtis also covered—both photographically and in his text—the Santa Clara pueblo, located on the Rio Grande River between the pueblos of San Juan and San Ildefonso. Like other pueblo dwellers, the Tewa and Zuni were primarily farmers, but today are best known for the beautiful pottery they produced—and continue to produce, each piece of hand-burnished, outdoor-fired pottery can be identified easily by originating pueblo. The clay is usually dug by older women from special (sometimes secret or sacred) locations, crushed, moisturized and left to cure. After pots are made by hand, they are burnished to a near mirror finish with smooth river stones, and then fired either in manure (for jet black) or bark (for red). Intricate incised designs also are added before firing. The process—at least for fine art pottery—has changed little over the years. The Pueblo people of both volumes had a richly developed religious life, much of which they kept secret from outsiders—particularly once the Catholic missionaries tried to extinguish those practices. The Indians vigorously resisted Spanish attempts to convert them to Catholicism (leading to the bloody Pueblo Revolt of 1680), but they eventually embraced a very loose version of Christianity while maintaining their traditional and rather secretive beliefs. Almost without question, the two volumes devoted to the pueblo Indians of New Mexico are the most popular of the entire series, and many of these faces show a bit of mischief.

Previous Page: Whyay-Ring. An unusual head-and-shoulders portrait of a Tewa Indian, wearing a felt hat with a feather in it, with the young Indian's focus slightly above the camera, ca.1905.
Library of Congress, Prints & Photographs Division, Edward S. Curtis Collection, LC-USZ62-112219

Right: Head-and-shoulders portrait of a dancer with an elaborate tablita headdress on the crown of her head. The young girl also is wearing a silver squash-blossom necklace, ca.1905.
Published in *The North American Indian*, Volume XVII.
Library of Congress, Prints & Photographs Division, Edward S. Curtis Collection, LC-USZ62-115816

X1709-05

Right: Pose-a yew. The facial features of many pueblo Indian men are either somewhat angular, as with this Nambe man, or are very rounded, c.1905.
Published in *The North American Indian*, Volume XVII.
Library of Congress, Prints & Photographs Division, Edward S. Curtis Collection, LC-USZ62-106250

Far Right: Oyegi-A-Ye (Frost Morning), was governor of the Santa Clara pueblo in northern New Mexico when this photograph was taken. The Santa Clara pueblo is one of the Eight Northern Pueblos, c.1905.
Published in *The North American Indian*, Volume XVII.
Library of Congress, Prints & Photographs Division, Edward S. Curtis Collection, LC-USZ62-130415

X1798-05

Right: Using sunlight streaming through his adobe room, this Zuni Indian bead worker is drilling holes in beads using a bone drill. This is one of the more unusual portraits taken by Curtis, as it was difficult to have enough light inside an adobe home for successful photos, c.1903. *Library of Congress, Prints & Photographs Division, Edward S. Curtis Collection, LC-USZ62-106757*

Far Right: Kó-pi ("Buffalo Mountain")— San Juan. This young man is dressed rather formally, with fur-covered braids, a bell and a dress shirt, c.1905. Published in *The North American Indian*, Volume XVII. *Library of Congress, Prints & Photographs Division, Edward S. Curtis Collection, LC-USZ62-121685*

COPYRIGHT
1903
BY E. S. CURTIS
X 825

Far Left: The ornaments worn by this young Zuni girl include strings of shell hishi beads and sterling silver necklaces with pendants. The round objects are coins, c.1903. Published in *The North American Indian*, Volume XVII.
Library of Congress, Prints & Photographs Division, Edward S. Curtis Collection, LC-USZ62-102041

Left: A Zuni pueblo girl, wrapped in a blanket, peers around the corner of the pueblo wall, smiling at the camera, c.1903.
Library of Congress, Prints & Photographs Division, Edward S. Curtis Collection, LC-USZ62-112232

Left: One of Curtis' most-reproduced Southwestern images shows a young Zuni man wrapped in a wool blanket, wearing a bandana. As with many Curtis portraits, the blanket likely conceals his modern clothing, c.1903.
Published in *The North American Indian*, Volume XVII.
Library of Congress, Prints & Photographs Division, Edward S. Curtis Collection, LC-USZ62-126293

Above: Zuni water carriers. Both of these women are wrapped in blankets and are wearing the thick-style traditional leggings. Each is balancing a large water pot on her head, c.1903.
Published in *The North American Indian*, Volume XVII.
Library of Congress, Prints & Photographs Division, Edward S. Curtis Collection, LC-USZ62-106266

Far Left: Si Wa Wata Wa. This old pueblo Indian's features and sharp eyes were of great interest to Curtis. The bandana, blanket and neutral background help make them stand out, c.1903.
Library of Congress, Prints & Photographs Division, Edward S. Curtis Collection, LC-USZ62-123309

Left: This young San Ildefonso girl, "Flower Morning," has a large pottery vessel balanced on her head. Curtis took a number of photos of the girl, who has a strong northern pueblo appearance, c.1927.
Library of Congress, Prints & Photographs Division, Edward S. Curtis Collection, LC-USZ62-117709

Right: A Nambe Girl. This young Nambe girl in her calico print dress and sly smile conveys the sort of innocence for which Curtis constantly searched, ca.1905.
Library of Congress, Prints & Photographs Division, Edward S. Curtis Collection, LC-USZ62-112210

Below Left: Head-and-shoulders portrait of Shiwawatiwa, a Zuni Indian, c.1903.
Library of Congress, Prints & Photographs Division, Edward S. Curtis Collection, LC-USZ62-111133

Below Right: Portrait of a Tewa boy, Okuwa-Tsire ("Cloud Bird"), San Ildefonso, c.1905.
Library of Congress, Prints & Photographs Division, Edward S. Curtis Collection, LC-USZ62-106260

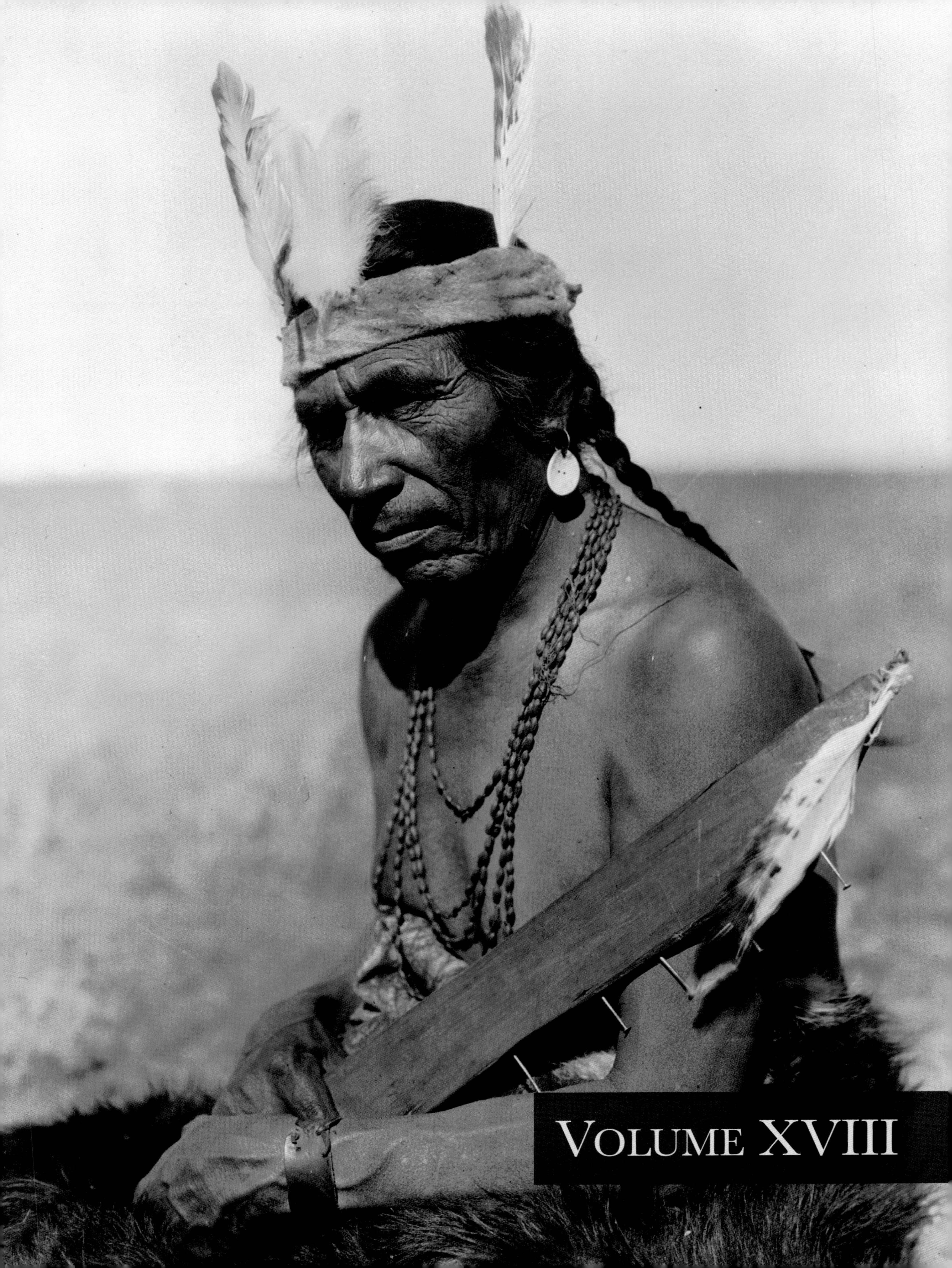
VOLUME XVIII

VOLUME XVIII

THE CHIPEWYAN. THE WESTERN WOODS CREE. THE SARSI.

FIRST PUBLISHED 1928

After the rush to produce three books in a single year, there was a two-year break until Volume XVIII was released. This was in part due to the loss of William Myers from the collaboration after the 1925 field season. Myers had been with Curtis since 1906. Curtis thanked him profusely in his introduction to volume XVIII for all his self-sacrificing work, which was accurate, since Myers regularly went for very long periods without pay as Curtis was always in financial crisis. In 1925, Curtis and Myers traveled to Alberta, Canada, to re-visit the Piegan and Assiniboin tribes Curtis had visited in 1899 with George Bird Grinnell. The intervening quarter century had not been kind to tribal life, and the pair found that government policies had very nearly stripped the Indians of their traditions. There was little to be gained, so they headed further north to visit several tribes that lived in the sub-arctic, including the Chipewyan and the Cree (in this case the western Woods Cree specifically), who were neighbors and bitter enemies. The Chipewyan lived in a land of long winters, originally thriving by hunting the region's vast herds of caribou. Eventually they became middlemen working with the White trading posts that popped up across Canada. The Cree also played an essential role in supplying the fur trade and became one of the largest and most important tribes in North America. The Sarsi were a small tribe that had became closely associated with the Blackfoot as a defense against their common enemy, the Cree. Curtis wasn't particularly enamored of the "modern Cree." He spoke of the frequent intermarriage between the Cree and fur traders that apparently had "no beneficial effect" on the descendants, "…for the modern Cree are decidedly inferior both in physique and in observance of the laws of hygiene."

Previous Page: Fat Horse with insignia of a Blackfoot soldier, c.1927, and probably dressed specially for this photo session. Curtis was dismayed at how heavily the Blackfoot confederation had assimilated into White culture by this date—a far cry from the traditional people he had photographed during his first Sun Dance gathering in 1900, ca.1927.
Library of Congress, Prints & Photographs Division, Edward S. Curtis Collection, LC-USZ62-106268

Right: Headdress of Matóki Society. Although you can see the subject's face in this profile portrait, Curtis was far more interested in the headdress. Nonetheless, the old man's face is quite communicative, ca.1927.
Library of Congress, Prints & Photographs Division, Edward S. Curtis Collection, LC-USZ62-101191

Above: Tsaassi-Mis-salla ("Crow with Necklace"), a Sarsi man, c.1927. By the time Curtis photographed the Sarsi, he was having a very difficult time finding any form of native dress that was not modern. As a result he relied heavily on blankets to help convey the sense of another time.

Library of Congress, Prints & Photographs Division, Edward S. Curtis Collection, LC-USZ62-119408

Above: Aki-tanni ("Two Guns"), another Sarsi, c.1927. Curtis reported only about 160 Sarsi living in the village at the time of his visit. Though members of the tribe insisted that not long ago there been many more, White visitors from the previous century noted a very similar population.

Library of Congress, Prints & Photographs Division, Edward S. Curtis Collection, LC-USZ62-127308

Above: Agichida, Assiniboin, c.1927. This Assiniboin, with a blanket over his denim shirt, exhibits strong Indian features that Curtis felt were characteristic of the type.

Library of Congress, Prints & Photographs Division, Edward S. Curtis Collection, LC-USZ62-136608

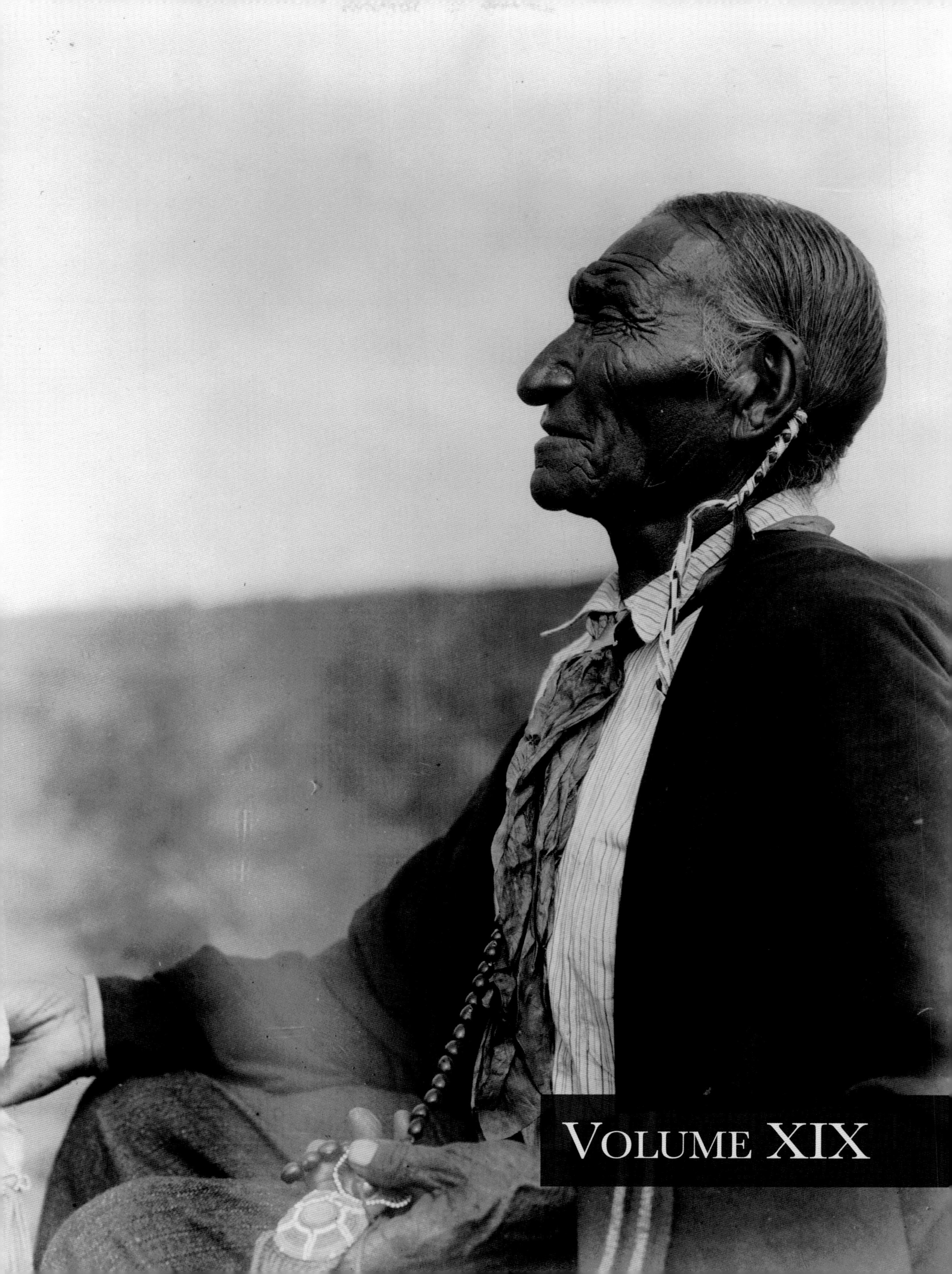
VOLUME XIX

VOLUME XIX

THE INDIANS OF
OKLAHOMA. THE WICHITA.
THE SOUTHERN CHEYENNE.
THE OTO. THE COMANCHE.
THE PEYOTE CULT.

PUBLISHED 1930

Edward S. Curtis enthusiastically embarked on his epic quest to record North American Indian culture because he realized that it was on the verge of disappearing. Unfortunately, by the time he neared home stretch—many years behind and tens of thousands of dollars in debt—his prophecy had largely become self-fulfilling, and he was bitterly disappointed by what he found in Oklahoma. Despite the fact that nearly a quarter of the entire U.S. Indian population lived in Oklahoma in 1926, the tribes of the Southern Plains were far removed from anything that resembled traditional. Most had been on reservations for decades and, in the case of the five "civilized tribes" (the Cherokee, Choctaw, Chickasaw, Seminole and Muskogee), had been relocated from their Eastern ancestral homes almost a century earlier. Significant numbers had already begun assimilating into mainstream America. By 1926 Curtis was searching for cultures that had not only disappeared, but were little remembered. One elder insisted to Curtis that what he wanted no longer existed. Even those who were children when Curtis first visualized *The North American Indian* were now on the verge of becoming tribal elders themselves, with little or no first-hand memory of how things had been. Further complicating matters was the relative wealth brought in by the oil fields. Curtis described Indians who had maids and chauffeurs, and who were part of the "idle wealthy." Curtis made no effort to cover the tribes comprehensively, writing first a historical introduction, then breaking the volume up by tribe. Editor Frederick Webb Hodge demanded a complete rewrite of the first draft of the text. In demanding the rewrite, Hodge leveled the charge that there was little usable information in the first draft. Curtis retorted that he couldn't get what wasn't there.

Previous Page: A Cheyenne Peyote leader, 1927. In a time of despair following the loss of much of their culture in the 19th century, there appeared several nativistic movements, such as the Ghost Dance of the 1880s–1890s and the Peyote cult—a mixture of Mexican, Indian, Christian, and Plains Indian symbolism. Peyotism has a strong following in the southern Cheyenne.
Library of Congress, Prints & Photographs Division, Edward S. Curtis Collection, LC-USZ62-106276

Right: Wife of Old Crow, Cheyenne woman, 1927. In this frontal, half-length portrait shot outside, Curtis posed the old woman in her beaded shirt, with hairpipe plate. He diffused the edges to soften the image.
Library of Congress, Prints & Photographs Division, Edward S. Curtis Collection, LC-USZ62-115823

Above: Rueben Taylor (Isotofhuts), Cheyenne man, 1927. Despite almost all odds, the Southern Cheyenne retained their traditional symbols of ethnic unity, the Sacred Medicine Arrows. These people can be found in Custer, Roger Mills, Canadian, Kingfisher, Blaine and Dewey counties of Oklahoma.

Library of Congress, Prints & Photographs Division, Edward S. Curtis Collection, LC-USZ62-121687

234

Above: A Wichita woman, 1927. The Wichita were unique among the Oklahoma tribes studied by Curtis in that they were native to the state. Most others had been relocated from elsewhere. Curtis said that the Wichita could be physically distinguished from the many Plains natives surrounding them because they were shorter, stockier and darker skinned.

Library of Congress, Prints & Photographs Division, Edward S. Curtis Collection, LC-USZ62-115822

Above: Henry, a Witchita, 1927. Although he gave him a blanket, Curtis made no attempt to hide the modern clothing or even the eyeglasses of this kind-looking older man. He also used outdoor lighting to give the man's features razor-sharp focus.
Library of Congress, Prints & Photographs Division, Edward S. Curtis Collection, LC-USZ62-136577

Right: A Witchita, 1927. Even though Curtis practically gave up trying to photograph the Oklahoma Indians in "native" garb, he posed this young Wichita in a headdress and classic stern Indian profile.
Library of Congress, Prints & Photographs Division, Edward S. Curtis Collection, LC-USZ62-136578

Above: Esipermi—Comanche, 1927. This half-length profile of Esipermi, and old Comanche, makes use of close-in cropping and high-contrast light. The shadows in the background add interest.

Library of Congress, Prints & Photographs Division, Edward S. Curtis Collection, LC-USZ62-136587

VOLUME XX

THE ALASKAN ESKIMO. THE NUNIVAK. THE ESKIMO OF HOOPER BAY. THE ESKIMO OF KING ISLAND. THE ESKIMO OF LITTLE DIOMEDE ISLAND. THE ESKIMO OF CAPE PRINCE. THE KOTZEBUE ESKIMO. THE NOATAK. THE KOBUK. THE SELAWIK.

PUBLISHED 1930

Almost as an antidote to Curtis' disappointing experience in Oklahoma was his 1927 field work for Volume XX, the final book in the series. Curtis, his daughter, Beth and new assistant Stewart Eastwood plied the Alaskan coastal waters in search of tribes. He was most taken with the Eskimos of Nunivak Island, off the southwestern coast of Alaska. Of the Nunivak Curtis wrote: "They are certainly a happy looking lot. At last, and for the first time in all my thirty years work with the natives, I have found a place where no missionary has worked." Curtis then added, "Should any misguided missionary start for this island I trust the sea will do its duty." Curtis finished by finding what he had largely been unsuccessfully looking for all those years and rediscovered why he began the project to begin with—an Indian culture that was relatively untouched by Whites. He went to Nunivak Island to study a culture that had so far eluded the destructive nature of contact with Whites. (In his introduction, however, Curtis stated that within a year of his visit the Nunivak lost nearly a third of its population.) Curtis acknowledged that he was covering but a small portion of the Eskimo culture, which stretched from the Aleutian Islands to eastern Greenland, but explained that there were great similarities in culture, and that his health would allow only the summer visit. The final volume, released in 1930, was barely noticed. The country, reeling from the 1929 stock crash, was in the full grip of the Great Depression, and book sales weren't an issue. Nonethess, for Curtis, the journey had finally ended. Curtis wrote, "It is finished." Fewer than 10 years after Curtis' visit, fundamentalist Christians would "save" the Nunivak natives, destroying much of their culture and burning many of their ceremonial artifacts.

Previous Page: Head-and-shoulders portrait of an Eskimo woman of the Arctic region, wearing a nose ring and labret, 1929. Her hooded parka is made of intestinal parchment. Women's parkas had extended hoods to allow the carrying of babies, and the tailoring and manufacture of the parka established a metaphysical identification with the animals on which these peoples relied for their existence.
Library of Congress, Prints & Photographs Division, Edward S. Curtis Collection, LC-USZ62-101193

Right: Noatak child, 1929. This small child, bundled in a huge parka for the portrait, was not happy about sitting still in a large, hot garment.
Library of Congress, Prints & Photographs Division, Edward S. Curtis Collection, LC-USZ62-107281

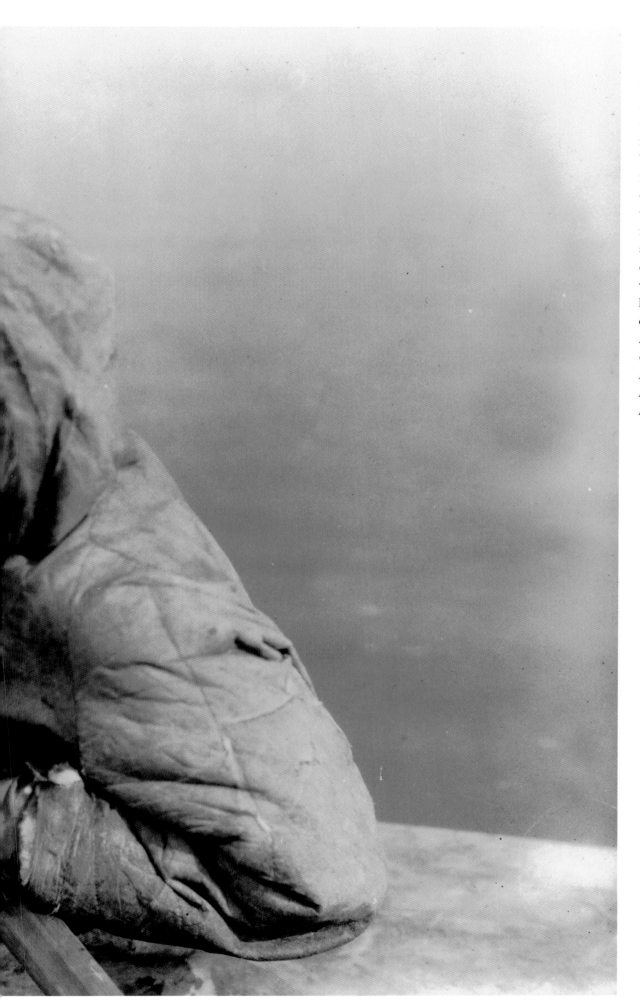

Left: Noatak seal-hunter in kayak, 1929. With few exceptions, the Eskimo was, and in many locations still is, a shore-dwelling sea hunter who is wholly carnivorous. The Eskimos were skilled in the making of the equipment necessary to win all the food they required from the sea and its margins, in a climate and a terrain which seem beyond the limits at which man could survive.
Library of Congress, Prints & Photographs Division, Edward S. Curtis Collection, LC-USZ62-107282; IH136937

Right: A Noatak family group, 1929. Curtis and his daughter, Beth, spent sixteen pleasant days on Nunivak Island among the Noatak Eskimos, people he described as happy and content. Indeed, of all the portraits appearing in the 20 volumes of *The North American Indian*, The Nunivak people are the most unguardedly happy. Curtis was pleased to have finally "found a place where no missionary has worked" and wasn't shy about saying he hoped things stayed that way. *Library of Congress, Prints & Photographs Division, Edward S. Curtis Collection, LC-USZ62-89847*

Left: Uyowutcha—Nunivak, 1929. This child is dressed in seal skins. Seals were of primary importance to the Nunivak and were hunted mainly in the spring and fall, when the animals migrated. Published in *The North American Indian*, Supplement to Volume XX. *Library of Congress, Prints & Photographs Division, Edward S. Curtis Collection, LC-USZ62-117002*

Above: Woman and child—Nunivak. Tradition dictated that when a child was born it was bathed in a wooden bowl and wrapped in a parka until the umbilical cord healed. A small fire was lighted and the baby frequently was named after the most recently deceased family member, c.1929. Published in *The North American Indian*, Supplement to Volume XX. *Library of Congress, Prints & Photographs Division, Edward S. Curtis Collection, LC-USZ62-107285*

Right: Like many Nunivak women, Dahchihtok has pierced ears and nose, as well as lower-lip piercings. It was thought the small sacrifice of pain for beauty was important, 1929.
Published in *The North American Indian*, Volume XX.
Library of Congress, Prints & Photographs Division, Edward S. Curtis Collection, LC-USZ62-13914

Far Right: Sea-bird maskettes, similar to the one worn by this man, were held in place with a wooden hoop that rested over the ears and balanced on the bridge of the nose. Many of these traditional masks and costumes were destroyed by Christian missionaries less than a decade after Curtis visited,1929.
Published in *The North American Indian*, Volume XX.
Library of Congress, Prints & Photographs Division, Edward S. Curtis Collection, LC-USZ62-13913

Above: This pair of grinning Nunivak boys pose in a kaiak (kayak). They were taught all the skills they'd need from an early age and were honored with feasts when they took their first game, c.1929. Published in *The North American Indian*, Supplement to Volume XX. *Library of Congress, Prints & Photographs Division, Edward S. Curtis Collection, LC-USZ62-46892*

Right: Kenowun—Nunivak. A smiling young woman sports her nose ring and beaded lip piercings—common adornments for Nunivak women at the time. Again, like so many of the Nunivak, the girl appears very happy, 1929. Published in *The North American Indian*, Supplement to Volume XX. *Library of Congress, Prints & Photographs Division, Edward S. Curtis Collection, LC-USZ62-74130*

Above: This young Hooper Bay youth is wearing an ornate fur hat and a pelt coat. Curtis found that the teeth of many Eskimos were darkened and in poor condition. c.1929.
Published in *The North American Indian*, Supplement to Volume XX.
Library of Congress, Prints & Photographs Division, Edward S. Curtis Collection, LC-USZ62-115023

Right: A King Island Eskimo man in a hooded parka is manually drilling an ivory tusk. The bow-style drill requires patience, but is highly effective. Although considered a portrait, the intent of this image is to highlight the activity, 1929.
Published in *The North American Indian*, Volume XX.
Library of Congress, Prints & Photographs Division, Edward S. Curtis Collection, LC-USZ62-13915

Right: Cape Prince of Wales man. Curtis was amazed—and pleased—in 1929 to find the Nunivak people still relatively untouched by modern civilization. Much of this unspoiled arctic paradise ended within a decade, however, c.1929. Published in *The North American Indian*, Supplement to Volume XX. *Library of Congress, Prints & Photographs Division, Edward S. Curtis Collection, LC-USZ62-119410*

Far Right: Jajuk—Selawik. This close-in portrait of a Selawik man contrasts the white fur of his parka with the dark intensity of his eyes. He has the appearance of what many would associate with that of an Eskimo. The Selawik inhabit the inland waterways of Alaska, 1929. Published in *The North American Indian*, Supplement to Volume XX. *Library of Congress, Prints & Photographs Division, Edward S. Curtis Collection, LC-USZ62-107918*

INDEX

Numbers in *italic* indicate text only.

Achomawi, 176
Acoma, 14, 203
Ah Chee Lo, 10
Angeline, Princess, 17
Apache, 7, 23, 24, 25, 26
Apsaroke (Crow), *52*, 63, 64, 65, 67, 69, 70, 72, 73, 74, 75, 76, 77, 78
Arapaho, *92*, 93
Arikara, 79, *80*, 84, 85, 86, 88, 90
Assiniboin, 56, 230
Atsina, 81, 82, 87

Bear's Belly, 85
Bird Rattle, 91
Black Eagle, 56
Bread, 78
Buffalo Mountain, 217
Bull Chief, 72

Cahuilla, 193
Calico, 62
Cayuse, 130–1
Chemehuevi, 200
Cheyenne, *92*, 104, 105, 106, 231, 233, 234
Chinook, *122*
Chukchansi, 183, 185
Clayoquot, 155, 158
Cloud Bird, 224
Comanche, 238
Cowichan, 142
Crow with Necklace, 228
Crow's Heart, 83
Cupeño, 195
Curley, 76
Curtis, Beth (daughter), *240*, *244*
Curtis, Clara (wife), *52*, *154*
Curtis, Florence (daughter), *170*, *182*
Curtis, Johnson A. (father), *10*
Czele Marie, 39

De Gazza, 35
Dieguéño, 196
"The Drink", 11

Eagle Child, 87
Elk Boy, 59
Eskimos, 239, *240*, 252, 253

Fast Elk, 61
Fat Horse, 225
Fiske, Frank, 20
five-view philosophy, *7*
Flatheads, *108*, 110, 111, 116, 117
Frost Morning, 215

Gardner, Alexander, 18, *19*
Golden Mean, *8*
goldtone, *16*

Grinnell, George B., *17*, *92*
Guptil (Gupthill), Thomas, *16*

Haida, *154*
Hamatsa, 143, 152
Harriman Expedition, *18*
Head Dress, 82
Hesquiat, 153
Hidatsa, *64*, 66
His Fights, 58
Hodge, Frederick W., *232*
Hollow Horn Bear, 58
Hoo-Man-Hai, 43
Hopis, 21, 22, 159, *160*, 161, 163, 164, 168
   snake priests, 166, 167
Hunt, George, *144*, 146, 149
Hupa, 169, 171, 177, 178, 179, 180

Isleta, 206

Jemez Indians, 205
Jicarillas, 27, 28, 29, 35, 36
Joseph, Chief, *122*, 128

Kato, 192
Kittitas, 120
Klamath, 174, 175, 181, 182
Klickitat, *108*, 114, 115
Kodak #1, *16–17*
Koprino, 148
Kutenai, *108*
Kwiakiutl, *144*, 146

Lake Mono, 198–9
Land of the Headhunters, *134*
Lean Wolf, 66
"Little Maid of the Desert", 21
Lone Tree (One Pine), 73

Maidu, 189
Makah, 156–7
Mandan, *80*, 83, 89
Maricopa, 42, 43, 44, 45, 47
masks, 147, 149
Mat Stams, 42
Medicine Root, 208, 209
Mike Shortman, 98
Miwok, 186–7
Mohave, 37, 38, 41
"Moki Melon Eaters", 15, 167
Monsen, Frederick, 22
Moon, Karl E., *20–1*
Moqui, 21
Mosa, 41
Muhr, Adolf, 20
Myers, William, *154*, *170*, *226*

Nakoaktok, 150, 152
Nambe, 214, 224

Named Woman of Many Deeds, 51
Nato, 161
Navajo, 8, 30, 31, 32, 33
Nespilim, 118, 119
Nez Perces, *122*, 124, 126, 127, 128
Noatak, 241, 242–3, 244–5
Nootka, *154*, 158
Nunivak, 246, 247, 248, 249, 250, 251, 254

O Che Che, 38
octopus hunter, 147
Ogalala Chief, 57
Old Bob, 172
Old Dog, 69
orotone, *16*
O'Sullivan, Timothy, *19*
Oz Sue, 25

Palmer, Frank, 18
"The Patient", 34
Pend d'Oreilles (Kalispel), *108*, 112, 113
Photo Secession movement, *17*
Pictorialism, *16*, *17*
Piegan, 91, *92*, 96–7, 98, 99, 106
Piki, 162
Pima, 18, 39
Plenty Coups, 65
Pomo, 188, 190
Porcupine, 106
Pose-a yew, 214
potlatch, 142
Pueblos, *24*, *38*, *202*, *212*

Qagyuhl, 147, 151
Qahatika, 6, 40, 48, 49, 50
Quilcene, 142
Quilliute, 133, 138, 139, 140

Red Cloud, 58
Red Dog, 53
Red Hawk, 60
Red Whip, 81
Reuben Black Boy, 94–5
Rinehart, Frank A., *19*, *20*
Rothi, Rasmus, *16*
Running Owl, 102–3

Salishan tribes, *108*, *134*
Sam Lopez, 180
San Ildefonso, 223, 224
San Juan, 217
Santa Clara, 215
Santa Ysabel, 196
Sarsi, 228, 229
Selawik, 255
Serrano, 197, 200
shamans, 143, 169
"Shoalwater Bay Type", 135

Shot in the Hand, 67
Si Wa Wata Wa, 222, 224
Sia, 201, 204
Sikyaletstiwa, *24*
Sioux, *12–13*, 15, 20, 53, 55
Sitting Bear, 84
Sitting Elk, 68
Skokomish, 136–7, 141
snake priests, 166, 167
Spotted Bull, 89
Stieglitz, Alfred, *17*
Sun Dance, *18*
Swallow Bird, 75

Taber, Isaiah, 19
Taos, 207, 208, 209, 210
Tewa, 9, 159, 163, 211
Three Eagles, 127
Tluwulahu, 151
Tolowa, 173, 180
Touch Her Dress, 112
Tsawatenok, 145, 149
Two Guns, 229
Two Kill, 96–7

Umatilla, 125, 129, 130
Upshaw, Alexander, *52*, *64*, 74

Vash gon, 36

Wailaki, 192
Walpi, *160*, 164, 168
Washo, 200
Werntz, Karl, 21
whalers, 155, 158
White Man Runs Him, 70
White Shield, 88
Wichita, 19, 235, 236, 237
Wild Gun, 100–1
Wilson's Photographics, 14
Wishram, 121, 123, 132
Wittick, Ben, *24*
Wolf, 71
Wounded Knee massacre, *13*, *52*

Yakima, 107, *108*, 109
Yanktonai, 54
Yaqui, 12, 46
Yellow Bone Woman, 55
Yellow Horse, 54
Yuki, 191
Yuma, 19
Yurok, 182

Zuni, 13, 216, 218, 219, 220, 221, 224